365 Toddler Activities That Inspire Creativity

That Inspire CREATIVITY

Games, Projects, and Pastimes That Encourage a Child's Learning and Imagination

Joni Levine, MEd

Adamsmedia
AVON, MASSACHUSETTS

For Lizzie, the daughter I used to only dream about.
You bring me more joy than I ever imagined.

Published by
Adams Media, a division of F+W Media, Inc.
57 Littlefield Street, Avon, MA 02322. U.S.A.
www.adamsmedia.com

ISBN 10: 1-4405-5074-3
ISBN 13: 978-1-4405-5074-4
eISBN 10: 1-4405-5075-1
eISBN 13: 978-1-4405-5075-1

Printed in the United States of America.

10   9   8   7   6   5   4   3   2   1

Contains material adapted and abridged from *The Everything® Toddler Activity Book, 2nd Edition*, by Joni Levine, MEd, copyright © 2012 by F+W Media, Inc., ISBN 10: 1-4405-2978-7, ISBN 13: 978-1-4405-2978-8.

Always follow safety and commonsense cooking protocol while using kitchen utensils, operating ovens and stoves, and handling uncooked food. If children are assisting in the preparation of any recipe, they should always be supervised by an adult.

Many of the designations used by manufacturers and sellers to distinguish their products are claimed as trademarks, including the restaurant and recipe names used in this book. Where those designations appear and Adams Media was aware of a trademark claim, the designations have been printed with initial capital letters. All rights to these trademarks are reserved by the various corporations who own these rights.

This book is available at quantity discounts for bulk purchases.
For information, please call 1-800-289-0963.

Contents

Acknowledgments

I have many people to thank for their help and support. Susan Holmes, for many ideas and lots of feedback. Ideas also came from Cathy Abraham, Terri Menzies, and Susan D. Smith. Robin Herbol provided artistic insight and a lot of support. I also wish to thank Barb Doyen, both agent and friend.

Introduction

As the parent or caregiver of a young child, you are an incredibly influential teacher. Toddlers are sponges—learning and growing from each game, book, and activity they're exposed to. Yet a lack of "playtime," a cutback on recess, and too much television are hindering children's development. The American Academy of Pediatrics strongly urges parents to limit children under two from watching television or using the computer. So how do you entertain a toddler all day? With creative activities!

Toddlers are naturally creative. They imagine blankets are tents and their fingers are puppets. Plus, encouraging this kind of creativity is a great way to help kids understand reality. Paul Harris, a developmental psychologist says, "The imagination is absolutely vital for contemplating reality, not just those things we take to be mere fantasy." According to the *Wall Street Journal*, more experts are studying the effects of imagination in children in the hopes that understanding how children's cognition typically develops will also help scientists better understand developmental delays and conditions such as autism.

The importance of creativity has taken center stage lately. In a 2010 IBM poll of CEOs worldwide, creativity was identified as the single most important leadership trait for success. Even though your toddler is decades away from being a CEO, he or she can still build a foundation for a lifetime of creative success with the activities in this book.

Fantasy play and make-believe will help your child in many ways beyond the boardroom, too. Pretend play is a safe way for children to express their feelings and try out new roles. Through make-believe, your child can learn to understand and convey strong feelings such as fear or anger. Make-believe also helps develop the ability to think symbolically, and that is essential to learning math and language.

As she chatters with her dolls or stuffed animals at a tea party, or he commands his toy cars to avoid (or maybe create) an accident, your toddler is strengthening his or her expressive language skills (the words the child speaks or signs). These skills will translate into school success and the ability to develop relationships.

Although the arts have received less attention in the public schools recently, research continues to support the importance of drama, music, and art. Individuals with greater self-expression are more able to think divergently and become creative problem solvers.

How to Use This Book

The activities in this book require little advance planning and few (if any) materials. And it does not matter where your child is developmentally; you will find ideas to meet her needs. The appendix is a useful guide, especially if you are seeking activities to promote a specific skill.

This book is designed to make it easy for you to find just the right activity for your child. Each activity includes a suggested age group and a time estimate. Activities are easy to follow, with a clear list of materials needed and step-by-step directions.

Activities that may pose any safety concern include a warning and/or suggestions for keeping your child safe. Some activities do use small items or potential choking hazards, such as Styrofoam and balloons. All activities in this book should be done under the direct and constant supervision of an adult. Carefully use your best judgment in selecting safe activities for your child.

Chapter 1
Toddlers 101

What Are Toddlers Like?

Toddlerhood, which encompasses the ages of eighteen months to three years, is an exciting period of your child's development. You have most likely noticed that she's growing rapidly and quickly acquiring many new skills and abilities. It may seem to you that just yesterday she was an infant, very passive and dependent on you. Now you can see that she is on the threshold of becoming a full-fledged individual.

Your toddler is truly caught in a time of transition. She is just starting to develop her own sense of self. At first, her only knowledge of her identity was that she was united with you. During the first few months of her life, she developed an attachment to you (and you with her). Her first relationship was with you. Now, however, she is slowly starting to see herself as a separate person, and soon she will develop new relationships.

Togetherness This time of becoming an individual includes separation and can be difficult for toddlers. However, when she knows that she can rely on you for love, comfort, and reassurance, she will be emboldened to take those first tentative steps away from you. In the meantime, you can assume you'll be doing all of the activities in this book side by side!

Separation Anxiety

Many toddlers begin to experience some feelings of separation anxiety anywhere from the eighth to twenty-fourth month. If your child is experiencing separation anxiety, she may become clingy and resistant to any separation. She may throw a temper tantrum and exhibit fear and anxiety around other people, even those who are familiar.

You may not be able to prevent your child from experiencing separation anxiety, but the way you respond can make things easier for all:

- ▶ Be sympathetic.
- ▶ Continue to be available to your child for comfort and reassurance.
- ▶ Whenever possible, avoid forcing her into situations that will be difficult.

When your child feels safe and secure, she will outgrow separation anxiety.

Emotional Volatility

As your toddler develops, she acquires many new skills. Along with physical and cognitive development, she is also maturing emotionally. You may find that your toddler's emotions are very close to the surface. Like flipping a light switch, she may go from happy and calm to fussy and agitated. At this age, she is likely to be easily overwhelmed and frustrated. Your calm, patient demeanor will be beneficial as you help her cope with and appropriately express her emotions.

Desire for Independence

You have probably noticed your toddler beginning to show a desire for independence. No longer completely dependent on you, she may even resist you during care-giving routines. She may start to insist, "Me do it," or "Let me try." Your child is developing autonomy. It is important that you give her opportunities to have some independence and to be sure to recognize both her efforts and her accomplishments. Many of the activities in this book will help you do just that.

Desire for Power

Along with this new desire for independence comes the wish for some degree of control and power. Your toddler is starting to learn that she can influence both the events and the people around her. Feeling a sense of autonomy and power is an important emotional milestone. Engaging her in activities that promote creativity and role-playing is a good way to show your child how to accept and manage these new emotions. Children who are restricted in this area can become doubtful of their abilities and may be reluctant to try things or act independently later on.

In an effort to assert this desire for autonomy and control, some toddlers may become defiant. They start to challenge limits and say "No!" to your requests. If you recognize that these behaviors are not made out of spite, you will be better able to manage them with patience and humor.

Limitations

Keep in mind that although your toddler is acquiring many new skills, she still has many limitations. She is quite egocentric, meaning that she has difficulty understanding the world from the perspective of other people. This makes sharing and empathetic behavior a challenge. She'll acquire these skills as she grows. Children repeat the behavior they see in you, so model sharing for her and practice empathy with dolls or stuffed animals.

Your toddler also has a long way to go in developing language skills. The second and third years of life are the times of the most rapid language growth. Some of the activities in this book take into account that some toddlers are still nonverbal, and will actually help to promote your child's language development.

How a Toddler Learns

Young children are naturally inquisitive and creative. It may seem to you that your toddler is compelled to explore and touch everything he can. His horizons are broadening daily, and there is much for him to discover. With so much that is still so very new, there will be no other time in his life that he will be this eager to learn. Capitalize on this enthusiasm, and nurture this inquisitiveness through both your attitude and the activities that you plan.

Sensorimotor Exploration

Young children learn best through direct sensory and movement experiences. If you wanted to teach your toddler about camels, you could try a few different teaching techniques. To your child, the information that a camel is a quadrupedal mammal that mainly resides in desert regions of Africa is meaningless. Nor is showing him a photo of a camel a very effective way to develop an understanding of what a camel is. Instead, you must engage your child in a quest to learn about camels. The best strategy would be to take him to the zoo, where he has the opportunity to see, hear, and touch an actual camel.

Should I Use Flashcards? Flashcards were once a very popular way to teach young children. Sometimes you will still see television demonstrations of "baby geniuses" who, with the help of flashcards, can name the state capitals or identify photographs of past presidents. You should know that these children have been drilled with memorization exercises and do not have a true understanding of the facts they are reciting. Instead, find creative and interactive ways to learn about subjects your child likes.

According to psychologist Jean Piaget, toddlers are in the sensorimotor stage of development. During this stage, a toddler learns best through direct, hands-on, concrete experiences. The capacity to learn through pictures, symbols, and abstractions does not develop until a child is six or seven years old. This is the reason that you will not find any worksheet-based activities in this book. Instead, each activity is geared to take advantage of the way toddlers learn best—by playing, by touching, and by having fun!

Other Ways to Learn

Your toddler learns in three main ways: through direct instruction, through imitation, and through sensorimotor exploration. Through demonstration and verbal directives, for instance, you can help your child learn basic skills, such as how to brush his teeth. You are a powerful role model for your child, and your actions speak louder than words. Some behaviors and skills, therefore, your child will learn by imitating you.

The most effective mode of learning, however, is through trial and error in sensorimotor exploration. Lessons that are relevant and that engage your child as an active participant will have the greatest impact.

How Creative Activities Help Your Child

You will not find any traditional, academic, rote-learning exercises in this book. But don't worry—neither you nor your child will miss them. Just about every activity described here is aimed to help your child develop in at least one critical area, and all of them are simply fun!

Play and imagination are the "schoolwork" of young children. Through play activities, your child is exploring and discovering. Play is the most effective and powerful way for young children to learn. Some scientists have found evidence that play can sculpt the brain and build denser webs of neural connections. When children play, they literally exercise their brain cells and make them expand and grow—a physical development that happens as your child learns.

Play activities engage your child and help her develop many skills, including vocabulary, problem solving, reading preparation, math comprehension, social skills, and more! The more creative and imaginative the play, the more your child will like it.

Is All Play Created the Same?

No. Although structured recreational activities and games do have value, the best activities are open-ended. Allow time for your child to choose and create her own play scenarios. She will benefit the most when she has the opportunity to explore the themes and ideas that are most important and relevant to her.

There are many different types of play activities, and each type addresses certain skills and promotes development. Here are just a few examples:

- ► **Cooking:** Develops math skills (counting and measuring), nutrition, and science concepts (prediction, cause and effect).
- ► **Art:** Develops creativity, emotional expression, symbolic representation, fine motor skills, large motor skills, cooperation, and spatial concepts.
- ► **Pretend play:** Develops social skills (cooperation, turn-taking, and sharing), language and vocabulary, imagination, and emotional expression.

- ▶ **Puzzles:** Develops problem-solving skills, abstract reasoning, shape recognition, and spatial concepts.
- ▶ **Block building:** Develops a foundation for more advanced science comprehension including gravity, stability, weight, and balance.

Choosing Appropriate Activities

Not every activity designed for toddlers will be right for your child. This is true for the activities in this book as well. You may find activities that are appropriate now and then come back later, as your child develops, to find other activities that are worthwhile. How do you choose appropriate activities for your child?

- ▶ Start with your child's interests and follow his lead. If he seems to enjoy spending time watching ants on the back porch, you may want to consider planning some activities about insect lore. If your child is afraid of clowns, avoid circus-related activities.
- ▶ Let your child's interest dictate how long an activity lasts and when to repeat it.
- ▶ Use your personal knowledge of your child's unique abilities to determine whether an activity is appropriate. If an activity is too complex, he may become frustrated. On the other hand, activities that are too simple may bore him.
- ▶ Although you want to choose activities that reflect your child's skill level, you don't have to worry about always keeping things easy. On occasion, go ahead and try an activity that poses some sort of challenge for your child. This doesn't mean something so difficult that he becomes confused or frustrated. Just keep an eye out for activities that allow your child to try something new, with your encouragement and guidance.

Age Ranges Are Only Guidelines

You want to choose activities that are a good match for your child's skills and abilities. Each activity in this book includes a recommended age range meant to serve as a general guideline. Some of the activities in this book are meant to engage young toddlers (beginning at eighteen months of age). Many other ideas presented here will still be enjoyable for children as old as four and five.

Top Ten Materials to Have on Hand for Toddler Activities

You'll find that some materials appear again and again in these activities. Here's a list of some of the most common:

1. **Crayons:** Remove the labels from crayons if necessary. For some younger children, fatter crayons work best.

2. **Construction paper:** Construction paper is very versatile. Be sure to keep a wide variety of colors on hand.

3. **Poster board:** Use poster board when you need a stronger, more durable paper.

4. **White craft glue:** You can also use rubber cement or school paste for most projects. Choose what works best for you and your child.

5. **Old magazines:** Old magazines are a wonderful source for collage and activity pictures. Nature, parenting, and home-living magazines are the best for this.

6. **Scissors:** In addition to adult scissors for you, purchase a pair of safety scissors for your child. If you wish, you can also find beginners' guiding scissors and fancy-edged scissors at school supply stores.

7. **Felt-tip markers:** Markers are useful for adding small details to projects. Some manufacturers even make washable markers.

8. **Food coloring:** This is handy for coloring homemade dough and various other craft materials. Please note: It does stain.

9. **Recycled household materials:** You can reuse materials such as egg cartons, yarn scraps, toilet paper tubes, and boxes for many activities.

10. **Nontoxic tempera paint:** Tempera paint is an easy paint for your child to work with. It has a nice, smooth texture and comes in many colors.

General Guidelines

There are ways for you to ensure that an activity is a fun and valuable experience for your toddler.

Keep It Short

Most toddlers have a very short attention span. He is too young to focus on an activity for any length of time and is apt to be easily sidetracked—especially from quiet activities or those that require him to remain passive, such as storytelling. Most activities presented here can be done in less than twenty or thirty minutes. If you want to plan a solid half-hour of activity time for your child, it is a good idea to set up two or three short activities rather than one longer one.

Be flexible and respond to your child. If you notice that he is losing interest in an activity, try to modify it to recapture his interest or simply move on to something else.

Guide Your Child

Toddlers like to feel competent, and that means they want to do things for themselves. This does not mean that you should set up an activity for your toddler and walk away. You need to be available to encourage and guide your child through all stages of each activity.

Although you do not want to "do" the activity for your child, it is acceptable to intervene if your child is having difficulty or showing signs of frustration. Gently make suggestions or ask questions to guide your child along. For example, if your child is having a hard time with a puzzle, you might say, "Why not try the blue piece?" or "What other piece could you try?" With your guidance, your child will be able to master many new skills.

Reduce Waiting

Waiting is especially difficult for the young child who does not clearly grasp time concepts. You cannot expect your toddler to be patient for long.

Avoid activities that call for children to be eliminated. (A game like musical chairs is an example.) Once the child is out, he is left, often frustrated and angry, to entertain himself.

Plan Ahead You can also avoid problems caused by waiting by preparing an activity in advance whenever possible. If there are props to be set up or game pieces to be cut, take care of that before you call your child over for the activity. That way your child can start playing right away.

Make Sure Your Child Is Involved!

The most valuable and fun activities are those that actively involve your toddler. Avoid activities that require your child to just sit back and watch. You can adapt most activities to enhance your child's involvement depending on his interest and skill level. For example, when an activity requires cutting out pictures, you can let your older toddler help you. Or you might let him stir the batter in a cooking activity or help set up the boundaries for a game.

Keep Activities Open-Ended

Whenever possible, look for activities that encourage your child to make choices. For example, the main goal of art experiences for young children is to promote creativity and emotional expression. There is very little value in having your child follow a rigid pattern to create something that looks just like the thing you or anyone else could make. Instead, encourage him to make what he wants and then tell you what he made. You'll see his interests and creativity shine through.

In the world of childhood art, boats may look like bananas, cats may have three eyes, and the sky can be orange. In the world of childhood games, someone may be "it" twice in a row, and it is okay to pin the tail on the donkey's head. When rigid rules and restrictions are lifted, the real fun begins!

Chapter 2

Activities for Morning, Noon, and Night

Morningtime Activities

If morningtime is a challenge in your family—trying to get children fed, dressed, and out the door—try some of these activities to help your child ease into the day with a positive outlook. Follow your child's lead; if she is not a "morning person," she will not enjoy too much stimulation early in the day.

Tiptoe

Young children will enjoy the overexaggerated sense of suspense as they pretend.

Activity for an individual child or a group

AGE GROUP: 18–40 months

DURATION OF ACTIVITY: 5 minutes

1. Encourage your children to creep or tiptoe throughout the house as they get ready for the day.

2. Try having them whisper or add to the excitement by pretending not to wake a sleeping giant or family member.

Felt Board Dress-Up

This activity gives your child a chance to use her creative fashion sense. It may also help alleviate the sometimes painful process of choosing clothing for the day. You can also try using this felt board at night, talking about the next day's weather and selecting what to wear in the morning.

Activity for an individual child

AGE GROUP: 18–40 months

DURATION OF ACTIVITY:
5 minutes

YOU WILL NEED:
- Felt board or large piece of cardboard
- Extra felt for making clothes

1. Get a felt board or simply glue some felt to a large piece of cardboard.

2. Attach cut-out shapes of children and provide the child with felt "clothing choices" to dress the figure. You can offer just a few options, or go all out—make party clothes, seasonal choices, and so on.

3. Encourage the child to create complete outfits, and talk about what the felt "child" might be doing that day.

Bend and Stretch

Here is a cute way to get your toddler up and moving in the morning. By reaching for imaginary objects, your child will be using his imagination, too.

Activity for an individual child

AGE GROUP: 18–40 months

DURATION OF ACTIVITY:
5 minutes

1. Teach your child this simple rhyme and the motions that correspond with it.

BEND AND STRETCH
REACH FOR THE SKY
STAND ON TIPPY TOES OH SO HIGH

BEND AND STRETCH
REACH FOR THE STARS
WAVE YOUR ARMS
BOTH NEAR AND SO FAR

2. Ask your child to fantasize about other things he could be reaching for.

Mealtime and Cooking Activities

Mealtimes can be a great way to interact with your toddler, have fun pretending, and make her feel involved. When you include your child in mealtime activities and preparation, she also is more likely to eat the food that you're serving. Additionally, cooking activities will help her learn about nutrition as well as science and math concepts such as fractions, measurement, evaporation, and more.

DIY Placemat

Your child will enjoy creating her own placemat that she can use at every mealtime. She may want to make one for each person in your family.

Activity for an individual child or a group

AGE GROUP: 18–40 months

DURATION OF ACTIVITY: 15 minutes

YOU WILL NEED:
- 12" × 14" sheet of poster board
- Crayons or markers
- Clear contact paper

1. Have your child decorate both sides of the poster board. Follow her lead to see where her creativity leads her—does she wants one side for breakfast and one side for dinner? One placemat for weekdays and one for weekends?

2. Use clear contact paper to laminate her creation.

Peanut Butter Playdough

You know your child is going to put Playdough in his mouth anyway, so you might as well make it taste good! Please note that honey is not safe for children under the age of one.

Variable Yield

Activity for an individual child or a group

AGE GROUP: 18–40 months

DURATION OF ACTIVITY:
10 minutes

YOU WILL NEED:
- 1 part peanut butter
- 1 part nonfat powdered milk
- 1 teaspoon honey (optional)

1. Mix all ingredients together.

2. Decide on a theme for what you'll make with the dough. Zoo animals? Pretend food? Vehicles? Jewelry?

Rainbow Toast

This is fun to make and fun to eat!

Activity for an individual child or a group

AGE GROUP: 30–40 months

DURATION OF ACTIVITY:
10 minutes

YOU WILL NEED:
- ½ cup milk
- Food coloring
- Cotton swabs
- 2 slices white bread

1. Divide the milk into 4 or more portions in small containers. An empty Styrofoam egg carton works well.

2. Help your child place a few drops of food coloring in each milk portion to create the colors she desires.

3. Have her use the cotton swabs as paintbrushes to paint colorful milk designs on the bread. Be sure they don't get too soggy.

4. Toast the bread under a broiler.

Mini Pizzas

Pizza may very well be the most popular food among children. Here is a way to involve your child in mealtimes and spark his creativity, too.

Activity for an individual child or a group

AGE GROUP: 30–40 months

DURATION OF ACTIVITY: 20 minutes

YOU WILL NEED:
- 1 canned biscuit
- 1 tablespoon tomato sauce
- 1 teaspoon grated mozzarella cheese
- Toppings as desired: pepperoni slices, onion rings, green pepper slices, etc.

1. Help your toddler pat the biscuit dough out into a circle, then help him spread on the sauce and cheese.

2. Let your child choose and arrange the toppings for his pizza. One idea is to use to pepperoni slices and a green pepper slice to make a smiley face.

3. Bake the pizza in a toaster oven or under the broiler until the cheese melts.

Playdough

This recipe produces a wonderful modeling dough that does not harden.

Make 1½ cups

AGE GROUP: 18–40 months

DURATION OF ACTIVITY: 10 minutes

YOU WILL NEED:
- ½ cup salt
- 1 cup flour
- 1 cup water
- 1 tablespoon cooking oil
- 1 tablespoon cream of tartar
- Food coloring

1. Mix all ingredients together and cook in a saucepan over a low heat.

2. Remove from the heat when the mixture starts to clump to resemble mashed potatoes.

3. While the mixture is cooling, knead in a few drops of food coloring. Store in airtight containers.

Transition Times

A chunk of every toddler's day is taken up by transition times—going from one routine to another. Though you may not think twice about them, they're common triggers for tantrums and misbehavior. These simple activities will help you keep your child motivated to move on to the next routine. Cleanup and chore times will also go more smoothly with these ideas that promote your child's imagination.

This Is the Way

Just about any activity or routine is more fun when you are singing.

Activity for an individual child

AGE GROUP: 18–40 months

DURATION OF ACTIVITY: 5 minutes

1. Make up different verses to the tune of "Pop! Goes the Weasel." Here's an example:

THIS IS THE WAY WE PUT ON OUR SHOES
PUT ON OUR SHOES, PUT ON OUR SHOES
THIS IS THE WAY WE PUT ON OUR SHOES,
SO EARLY IN THE MORNING.

2. Other potential verses might involve how to wash our face, wait for the bus, climb into bed, and so on. You can change the time of day as appropriate—to "late in the evening," for example.

Cleanup Is Fun!

It's true; most kids do *not* think cleanup is fun. Try these games to change his opinion!

Activity for an individual child

AGE GROUP: 30–40 months

DURATION OF ACTIVITY: 15 minutes

1. Explain to your child that all of his toys have homes, or special places where they belong. Then explain that he needs to make sure none of his toys get lost and must help each one find its home again. (It is helpful to have special places designated for your child's belongings. You may want to label shelves and cubbies with pictures to help your child match what belongs there.)

2. Option #1: Encourage your child to imagine the toys are going to sleep or back to their homes. Create a story about how the toys went on a safari adventure or into outer space.

3. Option #2: Guide your child by having him pick up items by category. For example, you might say, "Let's pick up all the red blocks first."

4. Option #3: Set a timer and have him try to speed-clean to beat the clock.

Helping Around the House

The toddler years are an in-between time in terms of development. Your child is no longer a baby, but she is not yet fully a big child, either. You will see your child's interest in, and possibly her insistence on, becoming a big girl. "Me do" or "Let me" may be a common request from her. You can give your toddler a chance to feel competent by enlisting her help with your chores. Toddlers love to imitate, and yours can learn new skills while bonding with you—and getting the house clean!

Washing Fun

Most toddlers enjoy water play, so they will truly love feeling as if they are helping you wash.

Activity for an individual child

AGE GROUP: 18–40 months

DURATION OF ACTIVITY: 15 minutes

1. The next time you are washing dishes or other items, set up a small bin with some soapy water.

2. Give your toddler a clean sponge, and let him wash his toys. Alternatively, let your child join you in hosing off the patio or even washing the car!

Pint-Sized Cleaning Tools

Your child's interest in imitation, pretending, and interaction with you may be all the motivation he needs to help out with the chores—especially if he has his own tools!

Activity for an individual child

AGE GROUP: 18–40 months

DURATION OF ACTIVITY: 20 minutes

1. Create a cleaning toolkit for your child. It can include a range of items: a small broom, mop, dust rag, pretend spray bottle, vacuum, and so on. To liven up the process, try cleaning certain kinds of items first, or racing against a clock, or imagining who could have made the mess in the first place.

Bathtime Activities

For some children, bathtime is very soothing and calm. For others, it's stressful, marked by battles and tantrums. It is not uncommon for children to resist the need to take a bath. Because of their vivid imagination, young toddlers often worry that they can slip down the drain. You can help make this a better experience with a very simple first step and just ensure that the water is a comfortable temperature. You will also find it helpful if you avoid rushing this routine and take the time to make things fun with these activities. To ensure the safety of your toddler at bathtime, eliminate all distractions and watch him closely.

Soap Crayons

This activity gives an opportunity for creative expression. Your child can use these crayons to draw on the tile or on herself!

Activity for an individual child

Makes 12 crayons

AGE GROUP: 18–40 months

DURATION OF ACTIVITY:
15 minutes to make and 2 days to set

YOU WILL NEED:
- 1 cup soap flakes or powder
- 3 tablespoons of water
- Washable tempera paint
- Ice cube trays or small paper cups (for molds)

1. Mix soap and water together to make a stiff dough that can hold its own shape. Add more soap powder or water as needed to reach the desired consistency.

2. Divide the mixture into 3 or 4 balls. Add a few drops of paint to each portion to create desired colors.

3. Press mixture into molds and let set for a few days before using as crayons in the tub.

Bathtub Finger Paints

Most toddlers love to get messy. What better place for a messy activity than the bathtub? They can express their creativity and wipe it clean.

Activity for an individual child

AGE GROUP: 18–40 months

DURATION OF ACTIVITY:
15 minutes

YOU WILL NEED:
- 2 tablespoons liquid soap
- 1 tablespoon cornstarch
- Food coloring

1. Mix all ingredients together for each color and store in covered containers. Mixture will last for a few weeks.

2. Let your child use the paints to paint on his body or on the tub tiles. When bathtime is over, the paint will rinse away.

Fishing in the Tub

Looking for toys under bathtime bubbles seems to happen all the time anyway. Make it an official fishing expedition!

Activity for an individual child

AGE GROUP: 18–40 months

DURATION OF ACTIVITY:
15 minutes

YOU WILL NEED:
- Toy plastic fish
- 1 small aquarium net

1. Simply add the toy fish to the bath water for your toddler to catch with the net. If you don't have toy fish, you can cut out some simple creatures from craft foam, or even a kitchen sponge!

Calming and Rest-Time Activities

Your toddler needs his rest, but it's often very difficult for young children to shift gears. They are unable to go from being active and wound-up to calm and restful without a transitional time. In other words, it is unrealistic to expect that your toddler will be able to go directly from chasing butterflies to a long and peaceful nap. Try to have a set routine with calming activities in place to assist your child in unwinding and preparing to rest. Fantasy and pretend activities can be very soothing if used in the right way.

Back Blackboard

Try this to help calm your child before bedtime. You can also massage your child's hands and feet this way.

Activity for an individual child

AGE GROUP: 18–40 months

DURATION OF ACTIVITY:
10 minutes

YOU WILL NEED:
• Body lotion, if desired

1. Ask your child to lie still on his stomach. Direct him to pay attention to what he feels.

2. Use your finger to draw on your child's back. For younger children, make shapes and spirals. For the older child, you can draw specific shapes, letters, or numbers and ask him to guess what they are. Use lotion for a variation.

3. Ask your child what he'd like you to draw on his back, then try to comply with the request.

Roll Up

Tucking in your child at bedtime can be part of a soothing ritual.

Activity for an individual child

AGE GROUP: 18–40 months

DURATION OF ACTIVITY:
5 minutes

YOU WILL NEED:
- Bed
- Extra blanket

1. Spread the blanket out on top of your child's made bed.

2. Have your child lie on top of the blanket on one side of the bed.

3. Ask your child to think of things he could pretend to be. Examples include: a burrito, a bug in a rug, a cocoon, and so on. Be sure the items are quiet and still.

4. Tuck the near side of the blanket over him and gently roll him across the bed until he is wrapped up in the blanket roll. Unroll your child before you leave him to go to sleep.

Monster Spray

Sometimes your toddler may take fantasy a bit too far. Help your child use his imagination to conquer his fears and get a good night's rest.

Activity for an individual child

AGE GROUP: 18–40 months

DURATION OF ACTIVITY:
10 minutes

YOU WILL NEED:
- 1 empty spray bottle
- Materials for decorating (markers, stickers, and so on)

1. Have your toddler decorate the bottle.

2. Tell the child that this is now a bottle of monster repellent. Let him spray wherever he thinks there could be monsters lurking!

Counting Sheep

Counting sheep is a time-honored way to cure insomnia. Try this cute game to help lull your toddler to sleep. Supervise closely if your child is still prone to putting things in his mouth.

Activity for an individual child

AGE GROUP: 30–40 months

DURATION OF ACTIVITY:
10 minutes

YOU WILL NEED:
• 8 to 10 cotton balls

1. Tell your child to pretend cotton balls are little sheep. Show him how he can herd them all on the pillow one by one. Perhaps they can hide under the covers, too!

2. Be sure to remind him that sheep are timid and that if he gets up or makes noise, the sheep will be frightened. If you are ambitious, you can use craft pom-poms and draw on eyes for more realistic sheep.

Chapter 3

Filling Up a Rainy Day

Get Moving!

Young children need plenty of opportunities to move around. You can usually meet this need by allowing your child to go outside, but what do you do when the weather is bad? Here are some creative indoor activities that will give your child a chance to burn off some of her pent-up energy.

Shadow Dancing

Here is a great way to get your child moving. Perhaps you can get the whole family to join in. Your child is free to express herself in many ways.

Activity for an individual child or a group

AGE GROUP: 18–40 months

DURATION OF ACTIVITY:
15 minutes

YOU WILL NEED:
- A bright lamp
- A light-colored wall
- Favorite music recording

1. Position the lamp in the middle of the room, leaving plenty of space between the lamp and the wall.

2. Turn on the bright lamp and darken the rest of the room. Aim the lamp directly at the wall. Stand your toddler in front of the lamp so that her shadow is cast clearly on the wall.

3. Put on the music and encourage your child to dance so that her shadow dances, too. For a cool-down activity, show your child how to use her hand to create simple shadow puppets.

Indoor Obstacle Course

When your child is stuck indoors, you will be happy to have an activity that helps her use her large motor skills and burn off steam. Stress to your child that this is a special activity that can only happen with your approval and supervision.

Activity for an individual child

AGE GROUP: 30–40 months

DURATION OF ACTIVITY:
30 minutes

YOU WILL NEED:
• Chair cushions
• Blankets
• Kitchen timer, optional

1. Find a safe place in your home to set up a miniature obstacle course. Set out pillows to use as stepping stones or hurdles. Use blankets to create tunnels. The path may also make your child navigate furniture, such as crawling under a table or climbing over the ottoman. If it won't make things too dangerous, consider timing her attempts and celebrate her fastest time.

Treasure Hunt

This game is easy to set up and will engage your toddler's sense of fantasy for a while.

Activity for an individual child

AGE GROUP: 30–40 months

DURATION OF ACTIVITY:
15 minutes

YOU WILL NEED:
• 1 roll of crepe paper (a long ribbon may be substituted instead)
• Favorite toy or prize

1. Thread the streamer in a trail around the room or house. Weave it around the couch, under the table, and so on—the goal is to make an interesting and challenging path for your child to follow.

2. Attach a favorite toy or a small prize at the end of the streamer for your child to find.

3. Give your child the loose end and have him follow along the path to find the treasure. Imagine where you are walking to find the treasure—a deserted island? A rainforest? Grandma's house?

Row the Boat

Your child can pretend they are rowing to a distant shore. Young children learn that they must take turns for this activity to work.

Activity for two children

AGE GROUP: 30–40 months

DURATION OF ACTIVITY:
15 minutes

1. Seat children on a soft floor, facing each other, with legs outstretched.

2. Have one child rest her legs over the other's. Once they are positioned, have the children hold hands.

3. Show them how to make a see-saw motion. One child slowly leans back, while the other child is pulled forward. Then the forward child leans back, pulling her partner forward. Encourage them to go slowly and smoothly and to not jerk each other. If one child is very young, she may need to work with an adult.

4. Encourage the children to row back and forth while singing "Row, Row, Row Your Boat."

Tea Party

This activity is fun for boys and girls. If your child doesn't like dolls, invite favorite action figures or stuffed animals. This does not have to be an elaborate party. You can use real materials, but pretend props work just as well.

Activity for an individual child

AGE GROUP: 30–40 months

DURATION OF ACTIVITY:
20 minutes

YOU WILL NEED:
• Paper plates, placeholders, party hats, play food, etc. (optional)

1. Let your child help you plan and set up the event. How should you make the invitations? What can you use for decorations? What will you serve?

2. Follow the level of your child's interest. You may simply need to put a few paper plates on a table, or your child may enjoy making placeholders, party hats, and so on.

3. Attend the party and be a good guest—enjoy the refreshments, and keep the conversation lively!

Rainy-Day Pictures

This fun rainy-day picture will help chase the blues away.

Activity for an individual child

AGE GROUP: 30–40 months

DURATION OF ACTIVITY:
20 minutes

YOU WILL NEED:
- Crayons
- 1 sheet white construction paper
- 3 or 4 large paper soufflé or baking cups
- White craft glue
- 3 or 4 pieces of yarn, each 3" long

1. Let your child use the crayons to color a picture of a rainy day.

2. Show your child how to make umbrellas. Fold the baking cups (which will double as umbrella tops) in half and glue to the rainy-day picture. Glue yarn "handles" to the picture underneath each umbrella top.

Window Clings

You and your child can make these decorations to suit any season or interest.

Activity for an individual child

AGE GROUP: 30–40 months

DURATION OF ACTIVITY:
25 minutes to make, 1 day to dry

YOU WILL NEED:
- Food coloring, various colors
- White craft glue in small bottles
- Sheet of clear flexible plastic, such as those used for transparencies

1. Mix food coloring with glue, a different color in each bottle.

2. Let your child squeeze the glue onto the transparency to create his picture or design. Filled areas work better than outlines. You can place a pattern under the clear sheet as a template for a design. Leave a hole at the top of your design for hanging the decoration later.

3. Let dry for 1 day and remove from plastic.

4. Thread a length of string or fishing line through the hole; hang decoration in front of a window.

5. To store, wrap securely in plastic wrap and keep in a cool place.

Indoor Snow Fun

Try these fun ideas when it is too cold to go out and play in the snow, or if you live in a warmer climate without snow. To add authenticity, give your child mittens and a scarf to dress up in while he is playing.

Activity for an individual child

AGE GROUP: 18–40 months

DURATION OF ACTIVITY:
45 minutes

YOU WILL NEED:
- White sheets
- Cotton balls
- White socks
- Instant potato flakes

1. Drape the white sheets over furniture and on the floor to create a wintry look to the room.

2. With your child's help, toss around the cotton balls and pretend that they are giant snowflakes.

3. Wrap pairs of white socks into balls and use them for a pretend snowball fight.

4. Put the potato flakes in a pan for sensory pretend play. If real snow is available, bring some in and let your child play with it in a contained area.

When Bad Weather Threatens

When bad weather is approaching, you may be facing more of a challenge than entertaining your child. It is common for young children to be frightened of storms. You need to set a good example—if you remain calm and nonchalant, chances are your child will stay calm as well. In addition, try these fantasy play activities. They will keep your child occupied and may even distract him from his anxiety.

Storm Sounds

Be sensitive to your child's fears. If he doesn't like loud noises, he may not like this activity. However, some children who are frightened of thunder may feel a greater sense of control when they can safely duplicate the noise.

Activity for an individual child

AGE GROUP: 18–40 months

DURATION OF ACTIVITY:
30 minutes

YOU WILL NEED:
- Audio recording of thunder
- Metal cookie sheets

1. Play the recording for your child. Discuss what he hears and try to figure out what is scary about the noises.

2. Show your child how to bang and rattle the metal cookie sheets to simulate the sound of thunder. Ask your child to come up with other ways to make thunder sounds, which may include banging on pots and pans or a toy drum.

Rain Sticks

Rain sticks have long been popular as musical instruments in other cultures. But you don't have to go to a fancy import store at the mall to buy one— your child can make one out of materials you have around the house. Many children find the sound of a rain stick to be very soothing.

Activity for an individual child

AGE GROUP: 18–40 months

DURATION OF ACTIVITY:
15 minutes

YOU WILL NEED:
- Crayons
- 1 cardboard paper towel tube
- 2 squares of tinfoil, large enough to cover the ends of the tube
- Masking tape
- 1 long pipe cleaner twisted into a loose coil
- ¼ cup dry rice

1. Let your child color the tube for decoration.

2. Fasten 1 tinfoil square on the end of the tube with masking tape. Leave the other end open until the tube is filled.

3. Help your child fit the pipe cleaner into the tube. Assist her in pouring in the rice.

4. Close the other end of the tube with the second square of tinfoil. Show your child how to tilt the stick back and forth to create the rain noise. Imagine all of the grass, flowers, and trees that are being watered during the rainstorm.

Let's Go Out

You don't have to always stay in when the weather is dreary. You won't melt, and there is a lot of fun to be had during a warm summer rain. Be sure to return inside if there is any lightning in the area.

Runny Pictures

Your child will enjoy livening up the yard with these beautiful but temporary creations. This works well with chalk too.

Activity for an individual child

AGE GROUP: 18–40 months

DURATION OF ACTIVITY:
20 minutes

YOU WILL NEED:
• Watercolor paint
• Paint brushes

1. Go outside before the rain comes or while it is just drizzling.

2. Let your child paint on the sidewalk or cement area to create any pictures he wishes.

3. Observe how the water makes the colors run.

Mini Streams

This is a great way to encourage your child to use observation and problem-solving skills, as well as his imagination.

Activity for an individual child

AGE GROUP: 12–40 months

DURATION OF ACTIVITY:
15 minutes

YOU WILL NEED:
• Sticks
• A patch of dirt or sand outside

1. Show your child how to use a stick or his finger to create a small trench in a patch of dirt where the rainwater can flow.

2. Encourage him to clear leaves to create mini rivulets.

3. Show your child how to lead the paths so that the water flows downhill. Observe how the trenches look after the rain has passed.

Design Your Own Storm Shelter

Once your shelter is built, you may wish to spend some cozy time in there snuggling or reading a story.

Activity for an individual child

AGE GROUP: 24–40 months

DURATION OF ACTIVITY:
30 minutes

YOU WILL NEED:
- Rain poncho or tarp
- Clothespins or duct tape

1. Help your child spread a poncho or tarp to create a tent or lean-to, either inside or outside your house. Drape the cloth over a piece of furniture, a large branch, or a fence.

2. Use clothespins or duct tape to fasten as needed. Talk about how you can stock the storm shelter with toys, books, and snacks to keep you busy while the storm passes.

Play Opposites: Make an Indoor Beach!

There is no better way to beat the stormy blues than to have a fantasy day at the beach in your very own home. Don't be surprised if the rest of the family wants to join in on the fun.

Beachcomber

Here is a fun twist on a simple scavenger hunt. You can alter the complexity of the challenge based upon your child's ability.

Activity for an individual child
or a group

AGE GROUP: 18–40 months

DURATION OF ACTIVITY:
15 minutes

YOU WILL NEED:
- Seashells (large enough so that they don't pose a choking hazard)
- Small plastic pails, one for each child

1. Hide a number of seashells in a room. Make some easy to find, and choose more challenging hiding places for others.

2. Give each child a pail, and encourage all of them to find as many shells as they can.

Beach Fantasy

This activity will help your child develop motor skills as she exercises her imagination. You can add to the fun by having your child dress in appropriate beach attire, such as a swimsuit and sunglasses.

Activity for an individual child or a group

AGE GROUP: 18–40 months

DURATION OF ACTIVITY: 15 minutes

1. Ask your child to pantomime various actions that take place at a beach. Possibilities include swimming, jumping over the waves, walking on hot sand, or surfing.

Indoor Beach

With a little effort and creativity, it is easy to transform your living room into a wonderful surfside paradise. You can always find fun, tropical-themed props at your local party supply store, too. Since you likely don't want to encourage sand or water play in the house, focus on creating the decorations and listening to the music.

Activity for an individual child

AGE GROUP: 18–40 months

DURATION OF ACTIVITY: 1 hour

YOU WILL NEED:
- Beach towels
- Scissors
- Brown construction paper
- Green crepe paper or ribbon
- Wall adhesive (such as Sticky Tack)
- Recording of beach-type music
- Beach-themed posters (optional)

1. Set up the beach towels as you would if you were at the beach.

2. Cut out a palm tree trunk from the construction paper, and cut sections of crepe paper for the fronds. Crease each frond into a wide "V" before attaching them to the trunk. Post the completed palm tree on the wall using the wall adhesive.

3. Hang any other themed posters or props, and play your favorite tropical music.

Fun with a Box

It is a common scenario: A young child excitedly tears through the fancy wrapping paper, ribbons, and bows. He opens the box and removes the year's newest and hottest toy. After a few minutes of play, he puts aside the toy and turns his attention and creativity to the toy he prefers—the box. In fact, boxes are wonderful, open-ended toys. Rather than running on batteries, they run on imagination!

Treasure Chest

Young children tend to find and collect little treasures. Many of these items may be meaningless and even bothersome to you, but they are dear to your child. Make this project with your child and give her a special place to store her treasures.

Activity for an individual child

AGE GROUP: 30–40 months

DURATION OF ACTIVITY:
20 minutes

YOU WILL NEED:
- White craft glue
- Wrapping paper or tissue paper cut to fit the outside of the box
- Cardboard shoebox with a lid
- Ribbons, buttons, fabric scraps, yarn, sequins, or any other crafty remnants available
- Mailing label
- Marker

1. Assist your child in gluing on the paper to cover the shoebox.

2. Provide her with many different materials to glue onto the box for decoration.

3. Apply the mailing label to the box and write your child's name on it. Find a special place to store the "treasure chest."

Box Train

There are so many dramatic play props that you can make with a box. This project is just a suggestion to help spark your own ideas. When cutting the rope, be sure that none of the sections are long enough to be a safety hazard.

Activity for an individual child

AGE GROUP: 18–40 months

DURATION OF ACTIVITY:
30 minutes

YOU WILL NEED:
- Three shoeboxes (or other small boxes open on top)
- Scissors
- Lightweight rope or string, cut into three 1' sections
- Tempera paint or markers
- Teddy bears, dolls, or action figures (to act as passengers)

1. Arrange boxes to form cars of the train. The front car is the engine—the open side of this box should be down, as the engine doesn't carry passengers. The other boxes are open side up.

2. Cut a small hole in the front and back sides of each box so that holes in all boxes line up.

3. Connect the boxes with the sections of rope. Knot the rope ends on the inside of each box to secure them. A rope in the front can be used to pull the train.

4. Let your child decorate the train with paint or markers. The train is then ready to carry its passengers. Talk about where the train is going and who's riding in it.

Shoebox Golf

This game tests your young child's motor skills and eye-hand coordination.

Activity for an individual child

AGE GROUP: 30–40 months

DURATION OF ACTIVITY:
20 minutes

YOU WILL NEED:
- Scissors
- 1 shoebox
- Crayons
- Masking tape
- 1 golf or Ping-Pong ball

1. Cut a hole in the center of the shoebox lid just a little bit bigger than the golf ball.

2. Invite your child to decorate the inside of the lid with crayons. (He can also decorate the rest of the box, but the inside of the lid is most visible as it is the playing field.)

3. Invert the lid and secure it over the empty box with a couple strips of masking tape. You want to be able to remove the lid to retrieve the ball.

4. Place the ball on the lid. Challenge your child to tilt the box back and forth and try to get the ball to fall in the hole.

Backward Upside-Down Day

The next time bad weather forces you to stay indoors with your child, why not make it into a special day? Try following the backward, upside-down theme throughout the day. Start the day by greeting your child with a "Good night!" Consider letting her wear some of her clothing backward. Maybe you can have breakfast as the last meal of the day. Here are some other ideas to get you started.

Backward Meal

Children of all ages will love the silliness of having a backward meal. Don't be surprised when you are asked to do it again next week.

Activity for an individual child or a group

AGE GROUP: 18–40 months

DURATION OF ACTIVITY: 30 minutes

1. If your family has assigned seats at the table, consider a shift. Let your toddler sit at the head of the table for this meal.

2. Of course, a backward meal must start with dessert! You can go the extra step by serving the pie à la mode upside down.

3. For the main dish, how about a backward sandwich or tortilla wrap? Put the meat and cheese on the outside with the bread and dressing in between.

4. Let your child suggest other silly ideas. She might decide to wear her napkin on her head instead of in her lap, or to use a fork for her pudding—why not?

Odd Pictures

Your toddler will have to be very imaginative to create this picture.

Activity for an individual child or a group

AGE GROUP: 24–40 months

DURATION OF ACTIVITY: 15 minutes

YOU WILL NEED:
• Paper and crayons

1. Ask your child to draw the back side or flip side of someone or something. What would it look like if our heads were backward? What does the back of a caboose look like? What's on the last page of her favorite book?

Chapter 4

On-the-Go Activities

Car-Travel Activities

"Are we there yet?" You may hear this mantra less often if you plan plenty of ways to occupy your children while you're gone. Set aside a play kit for your child to be used only for travel, so the toys stay fresh. Avoid small pieces that can be lost or become projectiles in an accident.

Silly Sounds

This is a lively game to play the next time your family takes a long drive.

Activity for a group

AGE GROUP: 18–40 months

DURATION OF ACTIVITY: 30 minutes

1. Players look out for animals or specific objects along the road.

2. When someone spots an animal or object, she identifies it by the sound it makes. For example, "I see a moo!"

3. Encourage your child to come up with creative substitutions. For example, she could say, "I see a choo choo," when she sees a train.

Magnetic Play

Here is a fun way to play with magnets when the fridge isn't around. When your child tires of pretend roadway play, he can also use the tray with magnetized letters and toys. Or, create magnetic dress-up dolls or even magnetic pictures of loved ones to arrange.

Activity for an individual child

AGE GROUP: 18–40 months

DURATION OF ACTIVITY:
20 minutes

YOU WILL NEED:
- Adhesive magnet discs
- Toy cars
- Cookie sheet (or other metal tray that magnets will stick to)
- Masking tape (optional)

1. Attach the magnets to the bottom of the toy cars.

2. Let your child drive the magnetized cars all around the tray.

3. If desired, help your child use masking tape to outline pretend roadways on the tray.

Tinfoil Modeling

Your child's creativity will have no limits with this easy activity.

Activity for an individual child

AGE GROUP: 18–40 months

DURATION OF ACTIVITY:
15 minutes

YOU WILL NEED:
- Aluminum foil or tinfoil

1. Provide your toddler with a sheet of aluminum or tinfoil.

2. Show him how to mold the foil into endless shapes and objects. Suggest a theme based on your travels—animals if you're going to a zoo, an umbrella if you're going to the beach, and so on.

In the Hospital

If your child is hospitalized or even bedridden at home, his activities will be limited. Remember, your child's imagination can take him farther than he could ever travel! When he starts to feel better, staying in bed can be difficult. Here are some quiet activities that you can bring to him while he recuperates.

Easy Collage

Being stuck in bed does not mean that your child cannot enjoy a simple craft activity. Be mindful that small items may pose a choking hazard if your child still puts things in his mouth.

Activity for an individual child

AGE GROUP: 18–40 months

DURATION OF ACTIVITY:
20 minutes

YOU WILL NEED:
- Clear contact paper, twice the length of the poster board
- 1 piece of heavy poster board or cardboard
- A variety of collage materials (felt, twigs, buttons, lace scraps, etc.)

1. Spread the contact paper flat on a table, sticky side up. Remove half of the protective paper.

2. Smooth the poster board over the sticky part of the contact paper. Fold the protected half over with the protective paper still on.

3. Let your child arrange the collage items on the poster board.

4. When he is satisfied, he can remove the paper from the top half of the contact paper and fix it on top of the design to keep the design pieces in place.

5. For a variation, you can skip the poster board and create a sticky sandwich with the contact paper used as both the base and top of the project.

Yarn Squiggles

Your toddler will be amazed at how the yarn will stick! To create a new design, he can just remove the yarn and start over.

Activity for an individual child

AGE GROUP: 18–40 months

DURATION OF ACTIVITY:
20 minutes

YOU WILL NEED:
- White craft glue
- 1 large sheet sandpaper (big enough to cover poster board)
- 1 sheet heavy poster board or cardboard
- A variety of yarn pieces in different colors and lengths

1. Glue the sandpaper onto the poster board to form a solid work surface.

2. Have your toddler arrange the yarn on the sandpaper. The yarn will stick on its own. If he's struggling for ideas of what to make, perhaps he'll want to imagine what he'll do when he's feeling better—play baseball, go to the playground, and so on.

Paper Chain

You can sometimes find paper chain kits in the store, but it is cheaper and more fun to make your own. These are a fun way to count down to an exciting event (grandma's visit? preschool?)—simply tear off a chain "link" per day!

Activity for an individual child

AGE GROUP: 30–40 months

DURATION OF ACTIVITY:
30 minutes

YOU WILL NEED:
- Scissors
- Lightweight bond paper in various colors
- Craft paste sticks

1. Cut out strips of paper 1" wide and 4" long. If your child is adept with safety scissors, he can help you.

2. Show your child how to apply a dab of paste with the paste stick and close each strip to make a link.

3. Help your child attach the links together.

4. When your child has completed a long chain, you hang it up to help brighten the room.

Activities to Do While Waiting

These activities are great fun whether you are waiting for a bus, sitting in a doctor's office, or just want to take a few minutes to interact with your child. These are also great activities to share with other people who care for your child.

Here Comes Daddy!

This is a great game to play when you are waiting to meet someone, like Daddy, in a public place. Depending on whom you plan to meet, this game might be called "Here Comes Grandma!" or "Here Comes Mommy!" Add an element of fantasy to this game by playing "Here Comes Santa Claus" or any other known or created fictional character.

Activity for two or more

AGE GROUP: 30–40 months

DURATION OF ACTIVITY: Variable

1. While waiting for Daddy, watch the other people who are walking past. Start the game by pointing out someone who is clearly not Daddy—the less like Daddy, the better. Enthusiastically say, "Here comes Daddy!"

2. The other person responds by pointing out someone who looks even less like Daddy and exclaiming, "No, here comes Daddy!"

3. Continue until Daddy arrives. You can reignite the game if he gets bored by guessing what Daddy will be wearing or carrying—make your guesses either realistic or very silly!

What's Their Story?

You can play this imagination-fueled game any way you choose. Just be sure that you are out of earshot of other people.

Activity for an individual child

AGE GROUP: 24–40 months

DURATION OF ACTIVITY:
15 minutes

1. Play this game any place where you can observe others from a distance. Shopping malls and airports are two great places.

2. Select a random person and ask your child to imagine about that person. Sample questions: Where do you think he is going? Why is he here? What did he do this morning? What is his job? Take a turn answering the questions and come up with silly responses.

When Fussiness Strikes

Even the most patient child is bound to get bored in a waiting room or on a long drive. Whenever you see that your child is starting to get fussy or you feel a tantrum could be around the corner, try one of these soothing ideas.

Instant Superhero

Your toddler's imagination is the only limit to this activity.

Activity for an individual child

AGE GROUP: 18–40 months

DURATION OF ACTIVITY:
5 minutes

YOU WILL NEED:
• Small blanket or towel

1. Show your child how to tuck a small blanket or towel into her collar to fashion a cape.

2. Encourage her to "fly" or act out any other superpower she can think of.

Real Finger Puppets

Add some pizzazz by taping some yarn or felt on for hair and clothing.

Activity for an individual child

AGE GROUP: 12–40 months

DURATION OF ACTIVITY:
15 minutes

YOU WILL NEED:
• Washable, nontoxic markers

1. Simply draw a face on each finger that you wish to use as a character. You may also wish to involve your child and use her fingers as well.

2. Create a simple play or act out a rhyme like "Little Miss Muffet."

Sightseeing Trip

This game requires everyone to use their imagination to keep the game fun and alive.

Activity for an individual child
or a group

AGE GROUP: 30–40 months

DURATION OF ACTIVITY:
15 minutes

YOU WILL NEED:
• You may use props if you
  wish

1. Set up a pretend vehicle, or use the one you're driving in. If you're inside, you can arrange chairs like a train or any other creative idea.

2. Set the stage by suggesting where you are going to visit. Some good places could be a jungle safari, a marketplace, or even your child's favorite playground.

3. Take turns pointing out what you "see:" "I see I giraffe!" "I see a giant twisty slide!" and so on.

Beach Activities

It may not take much to entertain *you* when you spend a day at the beach. Your toddler, on the other hand, might need more help. Once she tires of digging in the sand, she may be ready to call it a day. Try some of these activities to make a day in the sun fun for everyone.

Shell Tray

You can do this creative craft at the beach or take the materials home to make it later.

Activity for an individual child

AGE GROUP: 24–40 months

DURATION OF ACTIVITY: 45 minutes

1. Help your child a find a large clam, bivalve, or scallop half-shell. You can supply one if they are scarce on the beach you are visiting.

2. Help your child glue sand, shell bits, and other beach debris onto the outside of the shell.

3. Once dry, the tray can be used to hold small jewelry items or even other shells.

Beach Obstacle Course

All you need is a shovel and a stick to create a fun beach activity for your child.

Activity for an individual child or a group

AGE GROUP: 18–40 months

DURATION OF ACTIVITY: 15 minutes

YOU WILL NEED:
• A stick
• Small plastic beach shovel

1. With the stick, draw a winding line in the sand to create a path for your child to follow.

2. Use the shovel to create ditches or gullies along the path for your child to jump over. You can also build up mounds for her to climb over or walk around.

3. Have your child pretend that she is on a great exploration as she navigates the course.

Beach Towels

Here is a chance to let your child show her creativity and create something that she will enjoy using.

Activity for an individual child

AGE GROUP: 18–40 months

DURATION OF ACTIVITY:
15 minutes

YOU WILL NEED:
- Fabric paints in a variety of colors
- Pie tins (one for each color paint)
- Scissors
- Sponges
- Large light-colored towel

1. Empty each color of fabric paint into a separate pie tin.

2. Cut the sponges in beach-themed shapes (shells, starfish, fish, or suns).

3. Show your child how to dip the sponges into the paint and then press onto the towel to create a design.

4. Let the towel dry completely and follow the fabric paint manufacturer's instructions before using.

Beach Cast

This is a wonderful way for your child to preserve memories. Beach casts also make great gifts.

Activity for an individual child

AGE GROUP: 18–40 months

DURATION OF ACTIVITY:
15 minutes to prepare, 3 days to set

YOU WILL NEED:
- Small shovel
- Wet sand
- Pie tin or other small container
- Seashells, driftwood, and other medium-sized beach items
- Water
- Plaster of Paris

1. Have your child shovel wet sand into the container to fill it about one-third of the way.

2. Let her select items to add to the cast. Limit the items so that there is some space in between them.

3. Show your child how to press the items so they are securely stuck into the sand without being buried.

4. Mix water and plaster of Paris according to package directions.

5. Spoon the mixture over the sand and shells so that it reaches the rim of the container.

6. Let the cast dry for a few days, then gently remove from the container and rinse off.

Zoo Activities

There is so much to explore at the zoo. Take your time; your child will enjoy his trip much more if you allow him to linger where he wishes. Many zoos now have interactive features for young children. Seek out the exhibits that offer hands-on learning opportunities.

Move Like Me, Sound Like Me

Engage your child's sense of make-believe with this lively movement activity.

Activity for an individual child

AGE GROUP: 18–40 months

DURATION OF ACTIVITY:
1 hour

YOU WILL NEED:
- A trip to the zoo, or pictures of animals in a book or magazine

1. As you view an animal, ask your child to mimic how the animal moves and/or sounds. Good animals to imitate are monkeys, kangaroos, elephants, and the big cats.

Fur and Pelts

Let the beautiful animals at the zoo inspire your child's creativity.

Activity for an individual child

AGE GROUP: 18–40 months

DURATION OF ACTIVITY:
20 minutes

YOU WILL NEED:
- Construction paper
- Glue or paste
- Craft fur and felt with animal print patterns, cut in body part shapes

1. Ask your toddler to create his own animal using different fur and print patterns. What will he call this new species?

Museum Activities

Not too long ago, taking children to a museum was an exercise in frustration, given all of the interesting things they could look at but not touch. Fortunately, children's museums in many larger cities now recognize that children learn best through hands-on exploration. Even some of the larger traditional museums have added more interactive exhibits. You can make any museum more interesting to your toddler with these simple ideas.

What Is Happening?

Art exhibits do not have to be boring for your children. Encourage your child to use her imagination with this activity. You will also be developing her vocabulary and literacy skills.

Activity for an individual child

AGE GROUP: 18–40 months

DURATION OF ACTIVITY: 30 minutes

1. Find pictures that depict people. (Abstract or still-life paintings will not work for this activity.)

2. Ask your child to make up a story based on what she sees. Maybe your child will have a new idea about why *Mona Lisa* is smiling.

Art Inspiration

Let what your child sees at the art museum be an inspiration for his own creations.

Activity for an individual child

AGE GROUP: 18–40 months

DURATION OF ACTIVITY: 30 minutes

1. Find and discuss artwork of a particular style or artist.

2. Give your child the supplies he needs to create his own art imitating that style. Jackson Pollock or impressionist art is a good place to start.

Chapter 5

Out-of-the-Ordinary Art

Coloring

Coloring may be the most basic and common of all art activities for young children. Crayons are inexpensive and easy to transport and to clean. You will discover that you can spark your child's imagination by avoiding coloring books and templates and trying these open-ended ideas instead.

Tape Pictures

This is a simple way to encourage your child's creativity and fine motor skills.

Activity for an individual child

AGE GROUP: 30–40 months

DURATION OF ACTIVITY:
10 minutes

YOU WILL NEED:
- Masking tape
- Construction paper
- Crayons

1. Help your toddler tear the masking tape into smaller pieces and strips.

2. Have her put the tape onto the paper in any design that she wishes.

3. Let her color over the tape. Encourage her to color as much of the paper as possible.

4. Let her peel back the tape to reveal the picture.

Sparkly Pictures

Liven up your child's coloring projects with this easy idea!

Activity for an individual child

AGE GROUP: 18–40 months

DURATION OF ACTIVITY:
10 minutes

YOU WILL NEED:
- Crayons
- Dark-colored construction paper
- Paintbrush
- Salt water

1. Have your toddler color any design or picture she wants on a dark-colored sheet of construction paper. Remind her to press hard for the colors to show well.

2. Next, let your child use the brush to paint over her picture with the salt water. (Be sure to stop her before the paper becomes too soggy.) The crayons will resist the water. When the paper dries, the picture will sparkle wherever the salt remains.

Paper Bag Batik

This process will give your child's artwork a unique look.

Activity for an individual child

AGE GROUP: 18–40 months

DURATION OF ACTIVITY:
15 minutes

YOU WILL NEED:
- Scissors
- 1 brown paper bag
- Water
- Crayons

1. Cut the bag open so that it forms 1 piece of flat paper.

2. Help your toddler soak the bag in water and then squeeze the water out. Let the bag get wrinkled.

3. The wet bag will tear easily, so open it carefully and lay it flat.

4. Once the bag is dry, your toddler can color a design on it.

Black Magic

This classic activity still delights young children!

Activity for an individual child

AGE GROUP: 18–40 months

DURATION OF ACTIVITY:
20 minutes

YOU WILL NEED:
- White paper
- Crayons
- Black watercolor paint
- Paintbrush

1. Let your child color on the paper with crayons. Avoid dark colors such as black, brown, or gray. Show her how to press hard to make sure the crayon marks are heavy.

2. Once the picture is complete, your child will paint over the entire paper with the black watercolor paint. The original crayon drawing will resist the paint and show through.

3. For older toddlers, or with your assistance: Instead of using watercolor paint, help your child cover the picture with a thick layer of black crayon. (All crayon layers must be extra thick for this to work.) Scrape away patterns or designs using the side of a coin to reveal the vibrant rainbow colors underneath.

Rough Art

This activity will help your child express creativity and learn about textures.

Activity for an individual child

AGE GROUP: 18–40 months

DURATION OF ACTIVITY:
10 minutes

YOU WILL NEED:
- Crayons or chalk
- Different grades of sandpaper

1. Let your toddler explore coloring on the different textures of sandpaper.

Cupcake Crayons

Recycle and reuse old crayons! These homemade crayons are easy for small hands to hold, and they produce bright colors and patterns.

Activity for an individual child

AGE GROUP: 18–40 months

DURATION OF ACTIVITY:
30 minutes

YOU WILL NEED:
- Old crayons and crayon pieces
- Muffin tin
- Paper muffin or cupcake liners

1. Discard brown, black, and gray crayons.

2. Remove the paper from all crayons. Small fingers may need help with this.

3. Break remaining crayons into small pieces no more than ½" long. Supervise your child carefully to ensure she does not put any crayons in her mouth.

4. Distribute crayon pieces into muffin tins lined with liners.

5. Bake at 300°F until all the crayons are melted together.

6. When cool, remove the new cupcake crayons from the tins—peel off as much of the liners as you'd like and they'll be ready to use!

Painting

There is no end to the number of creative projects your child can complete with paint. Here you will find unique ideas that go well beyond a plastic palette and a little brush. Opt for nontoxic and washable paints whenever you can. As a general rule, tempera paints are best for young artists—watercolors come in less vibrant colors and tend to run, which might frustrate your child. You will also discover that you do not necessarily need store-bought paint for your painting projects!

Put Those Paintbrushes Away

Break away from the routine. Let your child's creativity be the only limit to the materials he can use to paint with.

Activity for an individual child

AGE GROUP: 18–40 months

DURATION OF ACTIVITY:
10 minutes

YOU WILL NEED:
- Paper
- Tempera paint
- Paintbrush substitute(s), such as condiment squeeze bottles, eyedroppers, fly swatters, spray bottles, makeup applicators, cotton balls, cotton swabs, string, tree bark, feathers, straws, pipe cleaners, or toothbrushes

1. Let your child paint using any number of paintbrush substitutes. He will find that each tool makes a different mark on the paper.

Wet Chalk Pastels

Using this new take on an old art material, these paintings will look like a professional artist was at work!

Activity for an individual child

AGE GROUP: 18–40 months

DURATION OF ACTIVITY: 15 minutes

YOU WILL NEED:
- Sidewalk chalk in various colors
- 1 cup water
- Dark-colored construction paper

1. Show your child how to dip the chalk into the water and let it sit for 1 minute.

2. Once the chalk is wet, show your child how to color on the paper—don't press too hard, or the paper will tear. The wet chalk will look like pastel paints.

Sticker Surprise

This activity will help develop your toddler's fine motor skills. Along with or instead of stickers, you can use return address labels, gummed paper reinforcers, or simply pieces of masking tape.

Activity for an individual child

AGE GROUP: 18–40 months

DURATION OF ACTIVITY: 15 minutes

YOU WILL NEED:
- A variety of adhesive stickers
- White construction or bond paper
- Tempera paint

1. Allow your toddler to choose the stickers that he wishes to use. Stickers with distinctly shaped outlines work best.

2. Show him how to attach the stickers to the paper in any arrangement that he chooses.

3. Paint over the entire paper, covering the stickers.

4. Once the paint is dry, help your toddler remove the stickers to reveal the sticker shapes.

Mirror Image Fingerpainting

This nifty process will let your child preserve his fingerpainting creations. You can have him paint directly on the table or onto a cookie sheet for easier cleanup.

Activity for an individual child

AGE GROUP: 18–40 months

DURATION OF ACTIVITY: 10 minutes

YOU WILL NEED:
- Finger paints
- White construction paper
- Cookie sheet (optional)

1. Have your child fingerpaint on a flat surface.

2. Press the white construction paper on top of the fingerpaint and rub—a mirror image of the design will transfer to the paper.

Ball Painting

It's like magic—when you open the box, you'll find a picture painted inside!

Activity for an individual child

AGE GROUP: 18–40 months

DURATION OF ACTIVITY: 15 minutes

YOU WILL NEED:
- Scissors
- White or light-colored bond paper
- Shoebox with a lid
- Masking tape
- Tempera paints
- Shallow pie tins
- Ping-Pong or golf balls

1. Cut a piece of paper to fit the bottom of the box. Tape it securely in place.

2. Pour small amounts of paint into the pie tins. Show your toddler how to dip a ball into the paint.

3. Have him place the paint-covered ball into the shoebox. Cover the box with the lid.

4. Let your child gently roll and shake the box around.

5. Remove the ball. Repeat with as many other balls and colors as desired.

Sculpting

The more your child can handle and manipulate materials, the more she will enjoy the project and the more she'll learn. Sculpture encourages your child to be creative, to see things in a new way, and to think "outside the box." Let these activities start you off in exploring this art technique with your child.

Three-Dimensional Sculpture

This project will turn your toddler into a mini-architect! She can use her problem-solving skills and creativity to make a 3D sculpture.

Activity for an individual child

AGE GROUP: 18–40 months

DURATION OF ACTIVITY:
10 minutes

YOU WILL NEED:
- White craft glue
- Masking tape
- Popsicle sticks
- Cardboard or poster board in various sizes and shapes
- Decorative materials such as foil or ribbon

1. Allow your child to glue and tape the materials together to create her own 3D sculpture. She can try to replicate a real item or simply make an abstract design.

Yarn Sculpture

Your child might love the ooey-gooey feel of the glue and the yarn as she molds this fun sculpture.

Activity for an individual child

AGE GROUP: 18–40 months

DURATION OF ACTIVITY: 2 hours

YOU WILL NEED:
- Yarn or cord in bright colors
- White craft glue
- Waxed paper

1. Have your child dip pieces of yarn in the glue to coat.

2. Let your child arrange the yarn pieces onto the waxed paper in any design she wants.

3. Allow the sculpture to dry for a few hours, and then remove it from the waxed paper. You may be able to hang it as a mobile for display.

Tissue Paper Sculpture

Your child will be developing fine motor skills and using her creativity with this activity.

Activity for an individual child

AGE GROUP: 18–40 months

DURATION OF ACTIVITY: 15 minutes

YOU WILL NEED:
- Colored tissue paper
- Small bowl
- White craft glue
- Water
- Cardboard

1. Have your child tear the tissue paper into small pieces. They do not have to be uniform in size.

2. In a small bowl, mix the glue and water in equal parts.

3. Show your child how to crumple up the tissue paper into wads. Dip each wad in the glue mixture and stick onto the cardboard.

4. Your child can add tissue wads onto a growing sculpture mound in this fashion.

Papier-Mâché

Papier-mâché is fun for all ages. Your young child will love the feel of the squishy paste. The best part is that the only limit to your creativity is your imagination. Be warned: This is a messy project!

Activity for an individual child or a group

AGE GROUP: 18–40 months

DURATION OF ACTIVITY: 2 days

YOU WILL NEED:
- Old newspapers
- 1 part flour
- 1 part water
- Mold or form (made from materials like wire, boxes, or balloons)
- Decorating materials

1. Have your child tear the newspaper into strips.

2. Combine the flour and water, adjusting proportions to achieve the consistency of very loose paste, like runny oatmeal. You may have to make more paste for progressive layers of your project.

3. Help your child dip each strip into the paste mixture and smooth it over the form. You will probably need to help your child squeeze the excess paste off the newspaper strip before removing it from the bowl.

4. Be sure that the entire mold is well covered with the paper strips. Let the layer dry before applying the next layer. Large or complex molds need multiple layers; small or simple shapes need fewer.

5. Once the sculpture is dry, it will be quite hard. You and your child can decorate it in many ways. Try using paint, markers, and glue with scraps of paper, feathers, or glitter.

Making Collages

There is no end to the number of materials that can be used for collages. Anything that will stick with glue is fair game. Let the ideas below be an inspiration for you and your child to create many variations.

Rice Collage

Your child will enjoy manipulating and gluing the rice. You will enjoy how bright the colors appear. This procedure also works well with dried pasta in distinctive shapes, such as macaroni or wagon wheels.

Activity for an individual child

AGE GROUP: 18–40 months

DURATION OF ACTIVITY: 30 minutes

YOU WILL NEED:
- Rubbing alcohol
- Food coloring in various colors
- Zip-top plastic sandwich bags (1 for each color used)
- Uncooked rice or pasta
- Waxed paper
- White craft glue
- Construction paper

1. For each color, mix ¼ teaspoon rubbing alcohol and a few drops of food coloring in a zip-top bag. Add ¼ cup of rice. Seal the bag and shake well.

2. Spread the rice on waxed paper and let dry.

3. Let your child use the glue to make designs on the construction paper. Sprinkle the rice over the wet glue to create a brightly colored picture. Let dry.

Natural Dye Collage

This activity will produce some very pretty fabric swatches. You may wish to use the resulting collage to make another project from the fabric, such as a kite or doll dress.

Activity for an individual child

AGE GROUP: 18–40 months

DURATION OF ACTIVITY:
10 minutes

YOU WILL NEED:
- Muslin fabric
- Natural materials such as berries, flowers, and leaves

1. Spread the muslin on the ground. Measure to the middle of the fabric swatch and mark the center line so that the fabric is divided in half.

2. Working on one half of the fabric, help your child place his chosen materials into any pattern or design he wishes.

3. Fold the fabric in half with the items inside.

4. Let your toddler pound the items through the muslin with a small hammer or mallet. Very young children can also stomp on the fabric to flatten the materials.

5. Open the fabric and brush away the remaining materials to reveal the collage design.

Other Art Media

Art is inherently creative. Look around your house on any given day, and you will find many items and materials to use for art projects. Recycled materials often make super art materials: Oatmeal boxes can become drums and margarine lids make great coasters. Try keeping a box of miscellaneous materials available for your child to create with.

Homemade Stickers

Does your child love stickers? Now you can make some from just about any image! This recipe is for adults to prepare. Let your child choose the images to use to make stickers.

Activity for an individual child

Makes ½ cup sticker glue

AGE GROUP: 18–40 months

DURATION OF ACTIVITY:
45 minutes

YOU WILL NEED:
- ½ cup vinegar
- 4 packets of unflavored gelatin
- 1 tablespoon peppermint extract
- Sticker materials, such as drawings, cartoons, or magazine pictures
- Small brush

1. Boil vinegar in a small saucepan.

2. Add the gelatin, then reduce to low heat and stir until gelatin is completely dissolved. Add extract and mix well.

3. Let the mixture cool before painting on the back of chosen images. Once dry, you will have stamps or stickers the child can use by moistening with a dab of water.

Bubble Prints

You will be amazed at the unique look of this project!

Activity for an individual child

AGE GROUP: 18–40 months

DURATION OF ACTIVITY:
15 minutes

YOU WILL NEED:
- Food coloring
- Bubble solution
- Pie tin
- Plastic drinking straw
- Paper

1. Mix a few drops of food coloring into the bubble solution. Pour solution into the pie tin.

2. Have your child use the plastic straw to blow bubbles into the solution. For young children, poke a few tiny holes near the top of the straw to keep them from sucking up any of the bubble solution.

3. Spread a sheet of paper gently on top of the bubbles to make a print.

Floating Art

Your toddler can create some unique pictures using this technique.

Activity for an individual child

AGE GROUP: 18–40 months

DURATION OF ACTIVITY:
20 minutes

YOU WILL NEED:
- Shallow baking pan
- Water
- Colored sidewalk chalk
- Cupcake liners or other small containers
- Construction paper

1. Fill the pan with water.

2. Help your child grate the chalk into powder. Place powder into the cupcake liners.

3. Help your child sprinkle the powder onto the water, letting her choose the colors, amounts, and patterns.

4. Have her spread a sheet of paper on top of the water to absorb the chalk design.

5. Hang the wet picture up to dry.

Spin Art

You may remember creating spin art paintings at the local amusement park when you were a child. Here is a simple homemade version to try.

Activity for an individual child

AGE GROUP: 30–40 months

DURATION OF ACTIVITY:
10 minutes

YOU WILL NEED:
- Paper plates
- Salad spinner
- Markers

1. Trim the paper plate if necessary before placing it directly into the spinner.

2. Crank the salad spinner to make paper spin.

3. Show your child how to hold the marker to draw on the paper while it spins.

What Remains

Your child will enjoy squeezing the glue to make different patterns, and she will be amazed to see her designs glitter and shine!

Activity for an individual child

AGE GROUP: 18–40 months

DURATION OF ACTIVITY:
15 minutes

YOU WILL NEED:
- Table salt
- Glitter
- Sequins or small pieces of foil (optional)
- White craft glue
- Construction paper or poster board

1. Mix salt and glitter in equal proportions. Add sequins if desired.

2. Help your child squeeze designs with the glue onto the paper. Swirls and squiggles look better than large puddles.

3. Show your toddler how to sprinkle the glitter mixture all over the glue design.

4. Shake the paper to adhere all loose glitter mixture possible to the wet glue. Tilt paper to discard remaining glitter mixture.

Crafts

Although crafts tend to be more structured, remember to let your child's originality rule whenever possible. Start with the basic format but encourage children to make their own alterations and variations to the pattern. So what if they paint the sky yellow, or the puppet has three eyes?

Sun Catchers

Here is a simple craft piece that your child will enjoy making—then you can display it at home, or give it to a grandparent as a gift.

Activity for an individual child

AGE GROUP: 18–40 months

DURATION OF ACTIVITY: 10 minutes

YOU WILL NEED:
- Hole punch
- Clear plastic lid, as from a deli container from the grocery store
- String
- Colored tissue paper or cellophane
- Scissors
- White craft glue

1. Punch a hole in the lid and attach string for the hanger.

2. Your toddler can help tear tissue paper into scraps. The cellophane will need to be cut.

3. Have your toddler glue the scraps onto one side of the lid.

4. When the lid is dry, hang in a sunny window.

Shrinky Things

You may remember the commercial version of this craft from when you were a child. Now you can make them at home in a flash!

Activity for an individual child

AGE GROUP: 18–40 months

DURATION OF ACTIVITY:
10 minutes

YOU WILL NEED:
- Scissors
- Thin sheets of Styrofoam (such as the butcher trays that come with hamburger or other meats, washed well)
- Hole punch
- Markers
- String

1. Cut the Styrofoam into desired shapes. Punch a hole at the top if you wish to hang the finished product.

2. Help your toddler decorate the shapes with the markers.

3. Microwave the creations for just a few seconds, and you will see them shrink!

4. Thread string through the hole if you wish to hang the finished project.

Magic Wands

Magic wands are the ultimate tool for make-believe play.

Activity for an individual child

AGE GROUP: 24–40 months

DURATION OF ACTIVITY:
10 minutes

YOU WILL NEED:
- Scissors
- Straw
- Stapler
- Cardstock
- Paste
- Glitter
- Ribbons

1. Cut 2 identical pieces of cardstock into a shape your child chooses: star, heart, and so forth.

2. Show your child how to add paste to one side of each cutout.

3. Have him sprinkle glitter on the paste and shake off the excess.

4. Sandwich the straw with the cutout shapes and staple together.

5. Help your toddler tie or staple ribbons onto the straw.

6. Encourage your toddler to use the wand to cast magic spells!

Chapter 6

Using the Five Senses

Sand Activities

Sand is a great sensory material for children to explore. It is versatile and easy to find, and it even changes properties when water is added. You do not need to have an elaborate sandbox or table for sand-play activities; simply use a plastic dish bin. Add a shovel, a funnel, and other simple tools, and your child will have all he needs. Good luck getting him to keep the sand in the container, though . . .

Pirate's Treasure

Your toddler will enjoy searching for the buried treasure! You may choose to think of other interesting things to bury.

Activity for an individual child

AGE GROUP: 18–40 months

DURATION OF ACTIVITY:
10 minutes

YOU WILL NEED:
- Gold spray paint
- Small rocks (large enough not to pose a choking hazard)
- Sandbox with sand

1. Paint the rocks and let them dry.

2. Hide the rocks in the sandbox and let your child dig for treasure!

Roadway

This activity combines the fun of sensory play with your child's imagination. You can also adapt this activity for any outdoor dirt area.

Activity for an individual child

AGE GROUP: 18–40 months

DURATION OF ACTIVITY:
20 minutes

YOU WILL NEED:
- Flat spatula
- Sandbox with sand
- Small toy cars and trucks
- Small blocks (optional)
- Toy or handmade mini road signs (optional)

1. Show your child how to use the spatula to draw roads and passageways in the sand.

2. Let him create the roadways and then drive the vehicles around.

Water Activities

Water play is soothing. Splashing and dipping in water is a stress reliever for both children and adults. You may find that your toddler is drawn to water, wanting to play in the sink or puddles. *Always* supervise your young child around water.

Boats That Float

Your toddler will enjoy helping to make these boats as much as playing with them. You can also use plastic container lids for small craft. You may see a small, rickety toy, but your child sees a cruise liner heading for exotic locations!

Activity for an individual child

AGE GROUP: 18–40 months

DURATION OF ACTIVITY:
15 minutes

YOU WILL NEED:
- Waterproof markers
- Thin sheets of Styrofoam (such as butcher trays that come with meat in the grocery store, washed well)
- Scissors
- 1 sheet white construction paper
- 1 small drinking straw
- Small blob of Playdough (see Chapter 2)

1. Let your child use the markers to color and decorate the Styrofoam.

2. Cut a small paper triangle with 2 horizontal slits.

3. Thread the paper triangle onto the straw to make a flag.

4. Place the blob of Playdough in the bottom of the tray to hold the flag.

Glacier Creatures

This is a good opportunity to talk about temperature and melting. Be sure to choose toys that are not a choking hazard.

Activity for an individual child

AGE GROUP: 30–40 months

DURATION OF ACTIVITY: 3 hours

YOU WILL NEED:
- Small toys
- Small clear plastic containers (Tupperware works well)
- Warm water

1. Place a toy in the plastic container.
2. Fill the container with water and freeze.
3. When the "glacier" is frozen, remove from the mold and add to your child's warm play water.

Natural Materials

Your toddler is naturally inquisitive, and he loves to explore. You don't have to look far to find fascinating sensory materials for him to play with. Don't be afraid to let him get dirty—that's half the fun!

Rock Painting

These make handy gifts as paperweights.

Activity for an individual child

AGE GROUP: 18–40 months

DURATION OF ACTIVITY: 20 minutes

YOU WILL NEED:
- Rocks
- Poster or tempera paint

1. Take your child outside and help him find rocks for painting. Large, smooth stones work best.
2. Let him paint his rocks with poster or tempera paint.

Finger Sketches

This activity can get a bit messy, so you may want to have your child do it outside or over a bin. Your child can create any picture he wants and erase his mistakes when he wants.

Activity for an individual child

AGE GROUP: 18–40 months

DURATION OF ACTIVITY:
15 minutes

YOU WILL NEED:
- Salt or cornmeal
- A flat tray with edges, such as a cookie sheet or shoebox lid

1. Put some salt or cornmeal on the tray to a depth of ⅛".

2. Show your child how to use his finger to create designs. You may wish to guide your child in practicing shapes and letters, too.

3. To clear the picture, the child can either gently shake the tray or just smooth over the design with his hand.

Mud Paint

Clearly, this is an outside activity!

Activity for an individual child

AGE GROUP: 18–40 months

DURATION OF ACTIVITY:
15 minutes

YOU WILL NEED:
- 1 cup of water, or more as needed
- Dirt
- Old spoon
- 1 sheet poster board

1. Either find some mud outside for your child to use, or help him make some mud by adding water to dirt. Use a spoon to whip the mud up to a creamy consistency. Add more water if needed.

2. With the spoon, place a blob of mud on the poster board for your child to fingerpaint with.

Playdough and Clay

Playdough and clay activities let your child use her imagination. She can preserve her creation, or she can squish it down and start all over again. Don't be surprised if your toddler is more interested in the process of working with this material than she is in creating something specific. Please see Chapter 2 for a basic Playdough recipe.

Playdough Cooking

Making pretend food is just one of many creative uses for Playdough. You may wish to use older kitchen utensils or pick some up at a garage sale.

Activity for an individual child

AGE GROUP: 18–40 months

DURATION OF ACTIVITY:
30 minutes

YOU WILL NEED:
• Playdough or craft clay
• Kitchen utensils

1. Provide your child with various tools and utensils for cooking up a pretend Playdough meal. Try these tools: garlic press for making pasta, cookie cutters, rolling pin, and measuring cups.

Playdough Textures

Enhance your child's Playdough fun by adding texture activities.

Activity for an individual child

AGE GROUP: 18–40 months

DURATION OF ACTIVITY:
30 minutes

YOU WILL NEED:
• Various tools and materials
  to add texture to the clay
• Playdough or craft clay

1. Provide your child with various tools and utensils for adding interesting patterns and textures to the Playdough, such as a meat mallet, potato masher, corrugated cardboard, or screen or netting.

Silly Putty

This project is messy, but the result is nicer than the commercial product. Sometimes this is also called slime or ooze.

Activity for an individual child

Variable Yield

AGE GROUP: 18–40 months

DURATION OF ACTIVITY:
15 minutes

YOU WILL NEED:
- 2 parts white craft glue or starch
- 1 part liquid starch

1. Mix together. If the mixture stays stringy, add a drop of glue. If it's too brittle, add more starch.

2. Chill for at least 3 hours.

3. Add either glue or starch as needed. Add a few drops of food coloring as desired.

Goop

This is a messy but fun sensory material.

Activity for an individual child

Variable Yield

AGE GROUP: 18–40 months

DURATION OF ACTIVITY:
10 minutes

YOU WILL NEED:
- 2 parts cornstarch
- 1 part water

1. Let your child use his hands to mix the ingredients together in a shallow bowl or container.

2. Have him explore what happens when he adds more water or cornstarch.

Mini Pots

Your child will develop fine motor skills as she explores ways to work with clay.

Activity for an individual child

AGE GROUP: 30–40 months

DURATION OF ACTIVITY:
15 minutes

YOU WILL NEED:
• Playdough or craft clay

1. Show your child how to roll the clay into a ball. Have her use her thumb to create an indentation in the middle and then pinch the sides out wider and higher to create a basic pinch pot.

2. Show your child how to roll sections of the clay into thin coils and then place the coils together to build the walls of a pot.

Bubbles

Bubbles are usually a good choice for entertaining young children. Toddlers especially love to watch them float, to chase them, and to pop them. All you really need is a nice breeze and a vial of bubble solution, but you can enrich bubble play with these activities.

Bubble Barber or Beautician

You can choose to do this activity in the tub or in the yard. This is a chance for your toddler to creatively explore many different looks.

Activity for an individual child

AGE GROUP: 18–40 months

DURATION OF ACTIVITY:
10 minutes

1. Run a bubble bath or create a foamy tub of water.

2. Encourage your child to pile on the bubbles to create hairdos and facial hair. You can start with the Santa Claus look and go from there.

Bubble Bonanza

This is a fun activity for a hot summer day. Consider having a bubble bonanza at your next family gathering.

Activity for an individual child or a group

AGE GROUP: 18–40 months

DURATION OF ACTIVITY: 20 minutes

YOU WILL NEED:
- Enough bubble solution to fill a small wading pool about 4" deep
- Jumbo-sized wands and other tools, such as hula hoops

1. Fill a small wading pool with bubble solution to a depth of 4". Careful supervision is needed should a child step into it, as the pool will be very slippery.

2. Gather large items for kids to use as wands. Try this fun idea: Have a child stand in the center of the pool. Place a hula hoop around her feet and slowly pull it up over the child to encase her in a bubble.

3. Have her pretend to be a sea creature, such as a mermaid or octopus!

Bubble Catch

Here is a fun and cooperative game that you can play with your young child. The best part is that you will have pretty pictures when you are done.

Activity for an individual child

AGE GROUP: 18–40 months

DURATION OF ACTIVITY: 15 minutes

YOU WILL NEED:
- Food coloring or tempera paint
- 2 small containers of bubble solution with bubble wands
- 2 sheets of light-colored construction paper or poster board

1. Add 1 or 2 drops of food coloring or paint to each container of bubble solution.

2. Let your child gently blow bubbles toward you. Hold out the sheet of paper to catch the bubbles. Take turns blowing and catching the bubbles.

3. When you are done, each player will have a picture made by the bubble residue.

Bubble Tools

You do not need to rely on the traditional wands that come with commercial bubble solutions. When you make your own bubble tools, you can control the size of the bubbles.

Activity for an individual child

AGE GROUP: 18–40 months

DURATION OF ACTIVITY:
10 minutes

1. Here are just a few ideas for making new bubble wands and tools:

- ▶ Twist together two pipe cleaners, then form them into a loop. Dip the loop into the bubble solution.
- ▶ Show your child how to hold a plastic berry basket and dip it into the solution and wave his arm around to make lots and lots of bubbles all at once.
- ▶ Tie a string to one loop of an unbroken six-pack holder and dip the whole thing into the bubble solution. Wave it around like a kite to get many, many gigantic bubbles.

Miscellaneous Sensory Materials

There are many materials that you can use for your child's sensory play. Remember, the most successful activities are ones where your child is directly involved. Perhaps these activities will inspire you to explore some new things with your child.

Shaving Cream Finger Painting

Toddlers love the feel of the shaving cream squishing through their fingers, and they enjoy the fresh smell as well. If your child can keep the mess contained on the pan, cleanup will be nice and easy.

Activity for an individual child

AGE GROUP: 18–40 months

DURATION OF ACTIVITY: 20 minutes

YOU WILL NEED:
- Nontoxic shaving cream (a nonmenthol variety)
- Large baking pan or cookie sheet

1. Squirt a blob of shaving cream on the baking pan in front of the child.

2. Encourage your child to smear and squish the shaving cream around, as he would with fingerpaint. Some children will dive right in, while others may be very reluctant to do this.

3. When your child is finished, simply wash the pan with hot, soapy water to remove the sticky shaving cream.

Scent Safari

Keep safety in mind while you do this activity with your child. Try to stick to nontoxic and all-natural products.

Activity for an individual child

AGE GROUP: 18–40 months

DURATION OF ACTIVITY: 20 minutes

1. Lead your child around the house and find interesting things to smell. Some suggestions include onions, lotion, cedar chips, shampoo, and spices.

Smelly Tacky Paintings

This is a fun project that will let your child explore different scents and textures while being creative.

Activity for an individual child

AGE GROUP: 18–40 months

DURATION OF ACTIVITY:
20 minutes

YOU WILL NEED:
- Spoon
- Water
- Light-colored construction or bond paper
- Different flavors of Jell-O (dark colors work best)

1. Help your child spoon a small amount of water onto the paper.

2. Let your child sprinkle the Jell-O powder on the wet patches.

3. Your child can then fingerpaint with these colors. She needs to try to be gentle so as not to rub through the paper. As she works, she will find that the consistency of the "paint" changes from gritty to sticky to slimy.

Texture Mitt

This activity is truly hands-on and promotes your child to explore and create with her senses.

Activity for an individual child

AGE GROUP: 18–40 months

DURATION OF ACTIVITY:
15 minutes

YOU WILL NEED:
- Cardstock or construction paper
- Scissors
- Glue
- Small fabric scraps of different textures

1. Cut the cardstock or paper into the shape of a hand.

2. Provide different fabric scraps for your child to use. Good examples include: satin, burlap, corduroy, seersucker, and twill.

3. Have her glue the scraps onto the paper to create a design.

Bubble Wrap Fun

Save the bubble wrap that comes with packages. You can also buy quantities of it fairly cheaply. Bubble wrap, like any other plastic, can be fatal if your child uses it to cover his face. Always use with direct supervision.

Activity for an individual child

AGE GROUP: 18–40 months

DURATION OF ACTIVITY:
30 minutes

YOU WILL NEED:
- Bubble wrap
- Scissors
- Tempera paint

1. Option #1: Let your child enjoy popping the bubbles. Show him how to roll the wrap up to pop more than one at a time.

2. Option #2: Spread the bubble wrap on the ground, and let your child walk and stomp on it.

3. Option #3: Cut out small squares of bubble wrap. Show your child how to bunch it up and dip it in the paint. Let him push the painted bubbles on the paper for an interesting effect.

Sensory Bottles

Sensory bottles tend to have a very calming effect on young children. They love to shake them and roll them and watch the contents swirl around.

Activity for an individual child

AGE GROUP: 18–40 months

DURATION OF ACTIVITY:
20 minutes

YOU WILL NEED:
- 1 or more (20-ounce) soda bottle(s)
- Water
- Liquid dish detergent, or
- Cooking oil and food coloring, or
- Light corn syrup, clear shampoo, or hair gel
- Small decorative items (such as sequins, buttons, or foil shapes)

1. Choose whether you would like to make a bubble bottle, wave bottle, or slow-motion bottle.

2. For a bubble bottle, fill the bottle ¾ of the way with water. Add 2 tablespoons dish soap.

3. For a wave bottle, fill the bottle ¾ of the way with water. Add 2 tablespoons cooking oil and a few drops of food coloring.

4. For a slow-motion bottle, fill the bottle with corn syrup, shampoo, or hair gel. Add the small decorative items of your choice.

5. Be sure to seal the bottles so that they do not leak and your child does not have access to small parts that he can choke on.

Music Activities

Little Red Wagon

Start by placing your child on your lap. Position her so that she is facing you and hold her securely. Tell your child that you are pretending to go on a wagon ride.

Activity for an individual child

AGE GROUP: 18–40 months

DURATION OF ACTIVITY: 10 minutes

1. Recite the following rhyme and follow the motions:

BUMPING UP AND DOWN IN THE LITTLE RED WAGON
BUMPING UP AND DOWN IN THE LITTLE RED WAGON
BUMPING UP AND DOWN IN THE LITTLE RED WAGON
OH (CHILD'S NAME) AREN'T YOU TIRED?

(BOUNCE CHILD ON BOTH KNEES SIMULTANEOUSLY)

ONE WHEEL'S BROKE AND THE ROAD IS BUMPY
ONE WHEEL'S BROKE AND THE ROAD IS BUMPY
ONE WHEEL'S BROKE AND THE ROAD IS BUMPY
OH (CHILD'S NAME) AREN'T YOU TIRED?

(BOUNCE CHILD ON KNEES, LIFTING ONE KNEE AND THEN THE OTHER)

TRY NOT TO LET THE WAGON TIP OVER
TRY NOT TO LET THE WAGON TIP OVER
TRY NOT TO LET THE WAGON TIP OVER
OH (CHILD'S NAME) AREN'T YOU TIRED?

(SWAY YOUR KNEES FROM SIDE TO SIDE)

Hula Dance

Start by making your own grass skirt. Hula dancing is great exercise too! Teach your child about how hula dancing is a creative interpretation of a story.

Activity for an individual child or a group

AGE GROUP: 30–40 months

DURATION OF ACTIVITY: 25 minutes

YOU WILL NEED:
- Colored crepe paper, streamers, or newspaper
- An old belt or ribbon
- Masking tape
- Recording of Hawaiian music

1. Help your child tear the paper into long strips. Attach them to the belt or ribbon. The more you use, the better the effect.

2. Put the skirt on your child and have her remove her shoes.

3. Play some Hawaiian music and show your child how to sway her arms and hips to the music.

Kazoo

This simple, homemade instrument sounds a lot like the real thing! Musical expression is a great way for a child to think creatively by inventing his own tunes.

Activity for an individual child

AGE GROUP: 18–30 months

DURATION OF ACTIVITY: 15 minutes

YOU WILL NEED:
- Pencil
- Toilet paper tube
- Markers
- 3" × 5" piece of waxed paper
- Masking tape

1. Use the pencil to poke a hole into one wall of the tube, approximately 1" from the end.

2. Let your child decorate the tube with markers.

3. Secure the waxed paper over the end nearest the hole you created. Wrap tape around the lip to keep the waxed paper taut.

4. Show your child how to play the kazoo by pressing the little hole and humming in the open end of the tube.

Microphone Craft

Bring out the star in your young child. Once he has a microphone, put on some music and let him ham it up. Let him be creative and watch his self-esteem soar.

Activity for an individual child

AGE GROUP: 18–40 months

DURATION OF ACTIVITY:
10 minutes

YOU WILL NEED:
- Tinfoil
- Toilet paper tube
- Black marker
- Small craft foam ball

1. Help your child mold the tinfoil over the paper tube so that both the bottom and sides are covered.

2. Have your child use the marker to color the craft foam ball.

3. Wedge the ball a third of the way into the tube.

Homemade Tambourine

What child doesn't enjoy making music? Let her create her own instrument with this easy project.

Activity for an individual child

AGE GROUP: 24–40 months

DURATION OF ACTIVITY:
15 minutes

YOU WILL NEED:
- 2 paper plates
- Markers or crayons
- 3 large jingle bells (avoid small items that could be a choking hazard)
- Stapler, glue, or masking tape

1. Have your child decorate the nonfood side of both paper plates. She can simply use markers or crayons, or take it to the next level with stickers, magazine cutouts, and so on.

2. Line up the paper plates so the decorated sides are face out. Seal halfway around the outside of the plates with a stapler, glue, or tape.

3. Add the jingle bells between the plates and continue sealing the rest of the way around the plates.

Drumstick

Since this activity is built upon the classic toddler pastime of banging on pots, your toddler may have already discovered this activity on his own. Close supervision is needed, and you should be sure to talk about why this is only an outdoor activity.

Activity for an individual child

AGE GROUP: 12–40 months

DURATION OF ACTIVITY:
5 minutes

YOU WILL NEED:
• Drumstick or drumstick substitution

1. Give your child a drumstick to use as a tapper. You can make one by super-gluing a wooden bead onto a dowel rod. Or in a pinch, you can use a wooden spoon or even a Popsicle stick.

2. Take your child outdoors and encourage him to tap on different things. Talk about what he hears. Possible items to tap include bricks, a tree trunk, and a rain gutter.

Visual Activities

Young children learn a lot about the world around them through their vision. These activities are sure to engage your child.

Invisible Pictures

Your child will delight in the magic effect of this picture.

Activity for an individual child

AGE GROUP: 18–40 months

DURATION OF ACTIVITY:
30 minutes

YOU WILL NEED:
- Lemon juice
- Paper cup
- White bond paper
- Cotton swabs

1. Put the lemon juice in the paper cup.

2. Let your child paint on the paper with the lemon juice, using the cotton swabs as paintbrushes. Let the design dry and become invisible.

3. Hold the paper close to a light bulb (without letting it touch). The design will become visible as the juice turns brown.

Invisible Pictures 2

Here is another easy way to create magic pictures.

Activity for an individual child

AGE GROUP: 18–40 months

DURATION OF ACTIVITY:
10 minutes

YOU WILL NEED:
- Bar of bath soap
- Light-colored construction paper
- Thick beginner's pencil

1. Let your child use the soap bar as a crayon to create a design on the paper. Remind him to press hard.

2. Show him how to rub the side of the pencil over the drawing to make it magically appear.

Bleeding Tissue Paper

Your child will love the brilliant colors of this project. You can also dye colors onto Easter eggs this way.

Activity for an individual child

AGE GROUP: 30–40 months

DURATION OF ACTIVITY:
20 minutes

YOU WILL NEED:
- Vinegar
- Paper cup
- Colored tissue paper
- White construction paper
- Cotton swabs

1. Pour a small amount of vinegar into a paper cup.

2. Have your toddler shred the tissue paper into small shreds. Don't worry too much about size and shape.

3. Show your child how to arrange the pieces of tissue paper on the white paper to create a picture or design.

4. Assist them in using a cotton swab to dab vinegar onto the tissue paper. Be sure they use enough to saturate the paper, but not so much that the vinegar runs all over the white paper.

5. Help your child to remove the tissue paper, leaving behind the brilliant colored picture.

Chapter 7

Dance and Movement

Dancing

Your toddler does not have to take lessons and learn fancy steps to dance. Encourage your child to be free and creative with her movements. Let her use her body to express herself. Don't be shy! Why not kick off your shoes and join in the fun?

Dancing Statues

This game will help your child develop listening skills and self-control while she has fun.

Activity for an individual child or a group

AGE GROUP: 18–40 months

DURATION OF ACTIVITY: 15 minutes

YOU WILL NEED:
- Music

1. Play music and encourage your child to dance. Randomly stop the music and ask the child to freeze a pose. As your child improves, you can ask her to hold the pose for longer periods of time.

Traffic Light

Your child can learn how to follow directions and develop self-control while she dances.

Activity for an individual child or a group

AGE GROUP: 30–40 months

DURATION OF ACTIVITY:
15 minutes

YOU WILL NEED:
• Scissors
• Construction paper in red, yellow, and green
• Paper plates
• Stapler
• Popsicle sticks
• Music

1. Cut construction paper the size of paper plates. Staple paper to plates and attach Popsicle sticks. These are your traffic signals.

2. Play music for your child to dance to. Hold up the different colored signs as she dances. When you hold up the green sign, she should dance fast. The yellow sign means dance slowly, and when you hold up the red sign, she should stop.

Dancing Partner

Dancing with a partner takes extra skill and coordination. Why not pair up your child with someone his own size?

Activity for an individual child

AGE GROUP: 18–40 months

DURATION OF ACTIVITY:
10 minutes

YOU WILL NEED:
• Music
• Large doll

1. Play music for your child to dance to. Provide him with a large doll to serve as his dancing partner.

Sock Hop

Turn back time and have an old-fashioned sock hop!

Activity for the whole family

AGE GROUP: 18–40 months

DURATION OF ACTIVITY:
20 minutes

YOU WILL NEED:
- Oldies music from the 1950s and 1960s
- Poodle skirts, leather jackets, and other timely apparel (optional)

1. Kick off your shoes and play some oldies to dance to. You can even show your children how to do some of the classic dances, like the Twist or the Swim.

Action Plays

Action plays are popular with young children. They are a great way to engage your child's imagination. Just about any story or rhyme can be adapted. Let these activities serve as an inspiration—maybe you can think of other ways to get your child to act out stories.

Jack and the Beanstalk

This is a fun activity to do right after reading the classic fairy tale by the same name.

Activity for an individual child

AGE GROUP: 18–40 months

DURATION OF ACTIVITY:
15 minutes

1. While reciting parts of the story, have your child imitate different parts of the action. Stomp around like the giant and tiptoe quietly like Jack.

Birds That Fly

This is a follow-the-leader activity. Much like Simon Says, the objective is to fool the player(s). For younger toddlers, just stick with the true directives.

Activity for an individual child or a group

AGE GROUP: 30–40 months

DURATION OF ACTIVITY: 15 minutes

1. Call out an animal and an action for your child to imitate. For example, when you call out, "Birds fly," your child should flap his arms like a bird.

2. There are many possible directives, such as frogs that hop, snakes that slither, or horses that gallop.

3. Try to fool him once in a while by calling out a silly directive. For example, say, "Fish hop." If you fail to trick him, he gets a turn being the caller.

Jack-in-the-Box

This short action play is sure to get your child's attention and bring some laughter as well. For younger age groups, you can instead play the song "Pop! Goes the Weasel." When the song gets to "pop," everyone can pop up. You may need to cue the child when it is time to do this by yelling, "Pop!" or raising your arms.

Activity for an individual child

AGE GROUP: 30–40 months

DURATION OF ACTIVITY: 15 minutes

1. While your child crouches on the floor, repeat the following rhyme in a slow and suspenseful way:

JACK-IN-THE-BOX, SO QUIET AND STILL. WILL HE COME UP?

2. The child springs up and shouts,

"OH, YES, HE WILL!!"

Rescue

Engage your child's imagination while helping him develop balance and large motor skills. You can change the theme of the rescue to suit your child's interest. Perhaps he can rescue the kitten from the dogs or the princess from the dragons.

Activity for an individual child

AGE GROUP: 18–40 months

DURATION OF ACTIVITY:
15 minutes

YOU WILL NEED:
- Assorted rags and stuffed animals

1. Place a bunch of rags in a small bag or basket.

2. Have your child scatter these around the floor.

3. Choose an object/prop to be rescued. This can be another rag, a stuffed animal, or something else. Toss this object into the center of the others.

4. Challenge your child to walk in and retrieve (rescue) this object without stepping on the others. You might tell him that the dragons are sleeping and that he needs to tiptoe in carefully.

Exercise-Based Activities

Many adults view exercise as an unpleasant chore. This is not so for young children. You will find that your toddler enjoys exercise just as much as any other movement or dance activities. In fact, she may be even more enthusiastic if she feels that she is doing a grownup activity.

Teddy Bear, Teddy Bear

This is an easy rhyme for your child to learn. By having her make up new versions, you will also be promoting her imagination and creativity.

Activity for an individual child

AGE GROUP: 18–40 months

DURATION OF ACTIVITY:
15 minutes

1. Teach this rhyme and corresponding movements to your child:

TEDDY BEAR, TEDDY BEAR, TURN AROUND.
TEDDY BEAR, TEDDY BEAR, TOUCH THE GROUND.
TEDDY BEAR, TEDDY BEAR, HUG ME TIGHT.
TEDDY BEAR, TEDDY BEAR, SAY GOODNIGHT.

Hopping Home

This exercise will also help your child learn to follow directions. If your child is learning how to count, you can ask her to hop a specific number of times toward the home base. Ask your toddler to pretend to be one of the many different animals that jump or hop.

Activity for an individual child
or a group

AGE GROUP: 30–40 months

DURATION OF ACTIVITY:
20 minutes

YOU WILL NEED:
• Area rug or chalk

1. Define a home base area. You can use an area rug or draw a square on the sidewalk with chalk. Also define a starting place for your child.

2. Your child must ask permission to hop to the home base. Each time, she gets to hop or jump once.

Track and Field

These tried-and-true games have been modified for even the youngest of athletes.

Activity for an individual child or a group

AGE GROUP: 30–40 months

DURATION OF ACTIVITY: 30 minutes

YOU WILL NEED:
- Carpet square or paper bag
- Tape or chalk
- Frisbee or beanbag

1. Add challenge to running races by adding hurdles. For the very young, use flat markers instead of raised obstacles to jump over. A carpet square remnant or even a paper bag can be used for this purpose.

2. Masking tape or chalk lines can be made to indicate a long or broad jump challenge.

3. Be creative. An old Frisbee can become a discus, and a beanbag makes a great shotput.

Cardboard Workout

Toddlers love to imitate. Here is a chance for them to pretend to be bodybuilders.

Activity for an individual child or a group

AGE GROUP: 30–40 months

DURATION OF ACTIVITY: 10 minutes

YOU WILL NEED:
- Scissors
- 4 paper plates
- 2 toilet paper tubes
- Crayons or markers

1. Cut small holes in the center of each of the paper plates. Fit the plates on the ends of the paper tubes to make barbells.

2. Let your child decorate her barbells.

3. Show your child how to imitate some bodybuilding poses as she lifts her "weights."

Sticky Balls

This silly activity encourages cooperation and helps develop motor skills.

Activity for a group

AGE GROUP: 30–40 months

DURATION OF ACTIVITY:
20 minutes

1. Have the children all bounce around in a defined area.

2. When 2 children meet, they stick together and bounce together.

3. Continue until all the children are stuck in 1 large ball.

Pop My Bubble

This activity promotes creative self-expression. Don't be afraid to switch roles.

Activity for an individual child

AGE GROUP: 30–40 months

DURATION OF ACTIVITY:
15 minutes

1. Ask you child to move like a bubble or balloon; inflate and float around.

2. Pretend to "pop" your child's bubble and ask her to move like a popped bubble or balloon would move. Perhaps she will zoom around or maybe she will collapse.

3. Encourage sound effects for extra fun.

Buzzing Bee

This activity is meant to help children with separation issues. You can dream up many potential variations. For example, you can be the moon and your child can be a spaceship. Or perhaps you are a gas station and your child is a car.

Activity for an individual child

AGE GROUP: 18–30 months

DURATION OF ACTIVITY:
10 minutes

1. You are the flower, so you sit or stand in one place. Your child is the bee who can buzz all around you and return for pollen!

Fun Walk

Children of all ages will want to try this activity. What other surfaces can you think of to include?

Activity for an individual child

AGE GROUP: 18–40 months

DURATION OF ACTIVITY: 10 minutes

YOU WILL NEED:
- Clear contact paper
- Bubble wrap

1. Tape a strip of clear contact paper onto the floor, sticky side up.

2. Stick a path of bubble wrap packing material onto the contact paper.

3. Have your child remove his shoes and socks before stepping on the bubble-wrap path. You may need to hold his hand to help him with balance.

Flying

This activity is best when your child has lots of room to move.

Activity for an individual child

AGE GROUP: 18–40 months

DURATION OF ACTIVITY: 10 minutes

1. Chant the following rhyme, and teach your toddler the movements to go along with the words:

THE AIRPLANE HAS GREAT BIG WINGS

(ARMS OUTSTRETCHED)

ITS PROPELLER SPINS AROUND AND SINGS

(SPIN ARMS)

THE AIRPLANE GOES UP

(ARMS UP)

THE AIRPLANE GOES DOWN

(ARMS DOWN)

THE AIRPLANE GOES THROUGH CLOUDS ALL OVER TOWN.

("FLY" AROUND)

Punchinello

Try this monkey-see-monkey-do activity the next time you have a bunch of young, restless children to entertain.

Activity for a group

AGE GROUP: 30–40 months

DURATION OF ACTIVITY:
15 minutes

1. Have children form a circle. Ask one child to stand in the center as the leader, Punchinello.

2. The children in the circle sing the following song:

WHAT CAN YOU DO, PUNCHINELLO, FUNNY FELLOW, FUNNY FELLOW?
WHAT CAN YOU DO, PUNCHINELLO, FUNNY FELLOW, FUNNY YOU?

3. The child in the center makes a movement. All the others imitate him while they sing:

WE CAN DO IT TOO PUNCHINELLO, FUNNY FELLOW, FUNNY FELLOW.
WE CAN DO IT TOO, FUNNY FELLOW, FUNNY YOU.

4. The child in the middle picks a new Punchinello. Continue until everyone has had a turn.

Using Props

When you add props to movement and dance activities, you enrich the activity and add interest. Also, by using props, you give your toddler further opportunities to develop fine motor skills.

Go Team!

No need to have a favorite sports team to cheer on—your child can be a cheerleader at any time.

Activity for an individual child

AGE GROUP: 18–40 months

DURATION OF ACTIVITY:
20 minutes

YOU WILL NEED:
- 2 sections of the daily newspaper
- Masking tape
- Scissors

1. First, create the pom-poms. Roll a section of newspaper into a tube shape. Tape the bottom securely and then cut the top half into strips.

2. You may wish to teach your child a simple cheer, such as "Go, team!" or "Two, four, six, eight, who do we appreciate?" Or you can just play marching music and let him swish and swirl the pom-poms.

A Thin Line

A piece of rope is all that is needed to help your child practice balance and coordination.

Activity for an individual child

AGE GROUP: 30–40 months

DURATION OF ACTIVITY:
15 minutes

YOU WILL NEED:
- Approximately 5' of rope

1. Stretch the rope out straight on the ground. Have your child practice walking along it like a tightrope walker. If you wish, you can have him use a balance bar.

2. Hold one end of the rope. Keeping the rope on the ground, wiggle it around and encourage your child to jump over it. If you don't think it will frighten your child, you can pretend that the rope is a snake.

Stick Horse

Watch your child's imagination take off when you help him make and then ride this easy stick horse.

Activity for an individual child

AGE GROUP: 30–40 months

DURATION OF ACTIVITY: 25 minutes

YOU WILL NEED:
- Scissors
- 2 sheets poster board
- Crayons or markers
- White craft glue
- Yarn
- Masking tape
- 3 paper towel tubes

1. Cut the poster board into 2 horse-head shapes.

2. Have your child decorate or draw a face on each piece of paper. Then let him glue on some yarn for the mane.

3. Using tape, attach the 3 towel rolls together to create the body. Put the 2 heads together back to back and attach them to the "body." Let your child finish decorating his horse, and he is ready to gallop away.

Parachute Activities

Activities with the colorful "parachute" used at many daycares, preschools, and camps are a great way to promote social interaction and cooperation. Children and adults can easily play together in these fun games. You can use a large sheet or light blanket if you do not have a parachute!

Popping Ball

This activity requires children to cooperate to get the ball to do what they want.

Activity for a group

AGE GROUP: 30–40 months

DURATION OF ACTIVITY:
20 minutes

YOU WILL NEED:
• 1 parachute or bed sheet
• Tennis or Ping-Pong balls

1. Have the children hold onto the edge of the parachute.

2. Drop one or more balls into the center of the parachute.

3. Ask children to pretend that the balls are frogs hopping on their lily pad.

4. Have children work together to get the ball(s) to move. Can they make the ball roll back and forth or around the edge? What do they need to do to get the balls to pop up in the air?

Parachute Pizza

This fun group activity will promote imagination and cooperation!

Activity for a group

AGE GROUP: 24–40 months

DURATION OF ACTIVITY:
15 minutes

YOU WILL NEED:
- Parachute or large flat sheet
- Pieces of yellow or white yarn for cheese
- Red paper plates for pepperoni
- Balls for meatballs

1. Place all the items on top of the parachute.

2. Ask participants to carry the "pizza" around carefully without losing any of the toppings.

Up and Down

Your child will be developing large motor skills as he works together with the rest of the group.

Activity for a group

AGE GROUP: 30–40 months

DURATION OF ACTIVITY:
20 minutes

YOU WILL NEED:
- 1 parachute or bed sheet

1. Have the children hold onto the edge of the parachute.

2. Instruct them to work together to pump the parachute up and down and to create a billowing cloud.

3. Have them release the parachute when it is fully extended to see which way it will float.

4. Alternatively, after the parachute makes a bubble, have the children squat or sit and tuck the parachute under their bottoms to create a mushroom.

Chapter 8

Let's Pretend

Props for Pretend Play

Your child's imagination can make a shoe transform into a trailer or a boat, while a margarine container becomes a swimming pool or a footstool for a doll. Sure, you can buy many toys and props that will add to your child's imaginative play. However, you can engage your child's imagination and creativity in making these simple props as well. Props for pretend play don't need to be elaborate.

Paper Bag Vest

Your child can decorate this vest to suit her imagination. It can be a cowboy vest, an astronaut suit, or perhaps a police uniform!

Activity for an individual child

AGE GROUP: 18–40 months

DURATION OF ACTIVITY: 15 minutes

YOU WILL NEED:
- 1 large brown paper bag
- Scissors
- Crayons, markers, or paint

1. If the bag has printing on it, gently turn it inside out.

2. Cut a straight line up the middle of the front of the bag.

3. On what was the bottom of the bag, cut a hole large enough for your child's head. Connect the large hole to the slit up the front.

4. Cut armholes on each side, positioned 2"–3" below the fold.

5. Provide different materials for your child to use to decorate the vest.

Shopping Bag/Purse

Toddlers love to tote their toys around. Here is a fun craft that yours can make. Always use caution when using long ribbons or cords that could pose a strangulation hazard.

Activity for an individual child

AGE GROUP: 18–40 months

DURATION OF ACTIVITY:
15 minutes

YOU WILL NEED:
- Scissors
- Old pillowcase
- Fabric paint
- 12" length of ribbon

1. Cut the pillowcase in half crosswise to create a shorter case.

2. Let your child decorate the pillowcase with fabric paints.

3. When the paint is dry, gather a small amount of fabric from each end of the opening. Tie the ribbon to the fabric to make the handle.

Jewels and Gems

This is as much fun to make as it is to play with. Mix this up in a large dish bin. Your child can use these to make-believe that he is royalty, or perhaps a pirate.

Activity for an individual child

Variable Yield

AGE GROUP: 18–40 months

DURATION OF ACTIVITY:
3 hours

YOU WILL NEED:
- 2 cups rock salt
- 6 to 8 drops food coloring
- ½ cup white craft glue
- Waxed paper

1. Mix the salt and food coloring together.

2. Add the glue and mix thoroughly.

3. Have your child mold into gem and jewel shapes.

4. Set on waxed paper to dry.

Doctor's and Nurse's Hat

These easy-to-make props will enhance your child's imaginative play.

Activity for an individual child

AGE GROUP: 18–40 months

DURATION OF ACTIVITY:
15 minutes

YOU WILL NEED:
- White bond paper
- White craft glue
- Scissors
- Bobby pins
- Cardboard circle 3" in diameter
- Tinfoil
- Crayons

1. Fold each sheet of bond paper lengthwise into thirds, then fold in half. Let your child glue the folds to form a band. Glue 2 together lengthwise to make a longer band. For the doctor's hat, the band needs to fit completely around your child's head. For the nurse's hat, the band only needs to go ⅔ of the way around. You may need to trim off excess.

2. To make the nurse's hat, fold up the corner of each end to form a triangle. Reopen slightly and attach to your child's head with bobby pins.

3. To make the doctor's hat, help your child cover the cardboard disc with the tinfoil to create the mirror. Let your child glue the disc on the front of the band. Secure the hat at the ends with glue.

4. Let your child decorate the hats with crayons.

Silly Glasses

Now your child can truly see the world through rose-colored lenses. Remember, these glasses are just for play and will not protect your child's eyes from the sun.

Activity for an individual child

AGE GROUP: 18–40 months

DURATION OF ACTIVITY:
15 minutes

YOU WILL NEED:
- Paper cup
- Poster board
- Pencil
- Scissors
- Colored cellophane
- White craft glue
- Hole punch
- 2 pipe cleaners or chenille stems
- Crayons

1. Use the paper cup to trace two circles on the poster board. Leave about 1" between them for the bridge.

2. Cut the glasses frame out in one piece. Let your child decorate the glasses with crayons

3. Cut out an inner circle in each eye, leaving a 1" rim.

4. Cut out cellophane pieces slightly larger than the eye holes. Help your child glue them in place to create lenses.

5. Punch a hole in the far end of each frame.

6. Loop and attach a pipe cleaner into each hole, then bend back the other end for the ear pieces. Be sure no wires are exposed on the pipe cleaners.

Common Pretend Themes

You will observe some common themes in your child's imaginative play. You can enrich these themes and extend her play by adding props and setting up a scenario for her to explore.

Restaurant Theme

Young children love to pretend to cook and eat food. As a bonus, you can reinforce manners and social skills while your child is playing.

Activity for an individual child

AGE GROUP: 30–40 months

DURATION OF ACTIVITY:
15 minutes

YOU WILL NEED:
- Table and chairs
- Paper plates, cups, and napkins
- Plastic tableware
- Poster board
- Crayons
- Notebook
- Plastic or real food

1. Let your child help set up the restaurant. Show him how to set the table.

2. Let your child create a menu on the poster board. You can have him color pictures of the food he wishes to serve. Alternatively, he can paste on magazine pictures.

3. Sit at the table and let your child take your order. Supply him with a small notebook so that he can pretend to write down your order.

4. If desired, let him serve you real or pretend food. Take turns ordering and serving.

Takeout Restaurant Theme

Mealtime is often a time when the entire family gathers together. Encourage everyone to participate in this game of make-believe as you're getting dinner ready.

Activity for an individual child

AGE GROUP: 30–40 months

DURATION OF ACTIVITY:
30 minutes

YOU WILL NEED:
- Takeout menus
- Large pad of paper
- Markers
- Backpack, basket, or other container (optional)

1. Using the props, help your child pretend that he is a delivery person. Have a family member "call in" an order and have your child "write" it down and then deliver it, using the backpack or basket. Switch roles.

Camping Theme

Why not consider expanding this theme with your child? It can be a fun family activity to camp out in the living room for the night. You could even make s'mores in the microwave for a bedtime snack.

Activity for an individual child

AGE GROUP: 18–40 months

DURATION OF ACTIVITY:
30 minutes

YOU WILL NEED:
- Small pup tent or large sheet
- 10–12 small sticks
- Scissors
- Red construction paper
- Sleeping bags (optional)
- Flashlights (optional)

1. Set up the tent. If you don't have one, drape a large sheet over a table.

2. Create a fake campfire. Arrange the sticks in a teepee shape. Cut out 2 flame shapes from the construction paper and prop them up among the stick structure.

3. Arrange sleeping bags under the tent or around the campfire.

4. Sit around the campfire and sing songs and tell stories. If your child will not be frightened, turn off the lights and use flashlights.

Medical Theme

Many young children are concerned and often fascinated about injury and illness. The subject of doctors and hospitals is something that your child may wish to explore. You can easily change this into a veterinarian theme; simply add a few stuffed animals and a pet carrier.

Activity for an individual child

AGE GROUP: 18–40 months

DURATION OF ACTIVITY:
15 minutes

YOU WILL NEED:

- Doctor's or Nurse's Hat (see this chapter)
- Fabric marker
- Old adult-sized, short-sleeved white shirt
- Dolls or action figures (to act as patients)
- Band-Aids
- Gauze or Ace bandages
- Rubber gloves
- Plastic syringe

1. Fit the hat onto your child. Make a lab coat by drawing a pocket and adding a name to the shirt.

2. Let your child put Band-Aids on her dolls and pretend to give them shots to make them feel better.

Dolls

Dolls are universally popular toys for your children. Toddlers love to imitate and try out the role that they see the most—that of adult caregivers! Playing with dolls gives your child the opportunity to pretend to be the mommy or daddy and also helps her or him to be less egocentric.

My Statue Doll

Your child can use this personalized doll as a prop in pretend or block play. For added fun, consider making a doll to represent his friends and members of the family.

Activity for an individual child

AGE GROUP: 18–40 months

DURATION OF ACTIVITY: 4 hours

YOU WILL NEED:
- Instant camera
- White craft glue
- Poster board
- Clear contact paper
- Scissors
- Air-hardening clay

1. Have your child stand facing forward in a simple pose. Compose the picture so that his head and feet are close to the edge but still in the frame. Make sure you use good lighting to get a clear photo.

2. Let your child glue the photo onto the poster board.

3. Help your child cover the photo with the clear contact paper. The contact paper should overlap the photo by ½" on each side.

4. Cut out the photo, following the contours of the body.

5. Have your child roll out a piece of clay into a disc the size of a half-dollar. This will form the statue's base.

6. Show your child how to stand the photo doll up in the clay base.

7. After several hours, when the clay is dry, your child can play with the statue doll.

Baby Bonnet Doll

This adorable craft also makes a nice gift idea.

Activity for an individual child

AGE GROUP: 30–40 months

DURATION OF ACTIVITY:
15 minutes

YOU WILL NEED:
- 1 little girl's anklet sock (with a frilly cuff)
- Cotton balls
- Ribbon
- Fabric paint

1. Show your child how to stuff the sock half full of cotton balls.

2. Tie the open end of the sock securely. If there is concern that the ribbon could be a hazard for your child, take extra steps to secure it with glue or a few stitches.

3. Fold back the cuff to create a bonnet.

4. Let your child use fabric paints to add on the facial features.

Give a Bath

This activity will help your child learn prosocial and language skills as she uses her imagination to practice caregiving.

Activity for an individual child

AGE GROUP: 24–40 months

DURATION OF ACTIVITY:
15 minutes

YOU WILL NEED:
- Shallow bin or wading pool
- Plastic, waterproof dolls
- Washcloths
- Shampoo or soap

1. Fill bin with warm water.

2. Show your child how to bathe the dolls.

Handkerchief Doll

Here is a cute doll that is easy to make. Skip the ribbons if your child is still putting things in his mouth.

Activity for an individual child

AGE GROUP: 30–40 months

DURATION OF ACTIVITY:
15 minutes

YOU WILL NEED:
• Handkerchief or square piece of fabric
• Small Styrofoam ball or tennis ball
• 3 rubber bands
• Ribbon (optional)
• Fabric paint

1. Fold the handkerchief in half.

2. Have your child place the ball inside, positioning it at the center of the fold.

3. Secure a rubber band under the ball to create a head.

4. Help your child gather the fabric from each top corner to form points.

5. Secure each point with a rubber band to create arms.

6. Tie a ribbon around the neck and arm joints.

7. Let your child paint on a face and other features with the fabric paint.

Block Building

There are many ways that your child will benefit from block play. Blocks are an open-ended material, meaning that your child is free to create and imagine whatever she dreams of. When she is building with blocks, she is learning problem solving and mathematical concepts including spatial relationships, balance, and shapes.

Block City

Help set the stage for many block-building adventures.

Activity for an individual child

AGE GROUP: 18–40 months

DURATION OF ACTIVITY:
30 minutes

YOU WILL NEED:
- Plastic tarp or old plastic tablecloth
- Ruler
- Permanent markers
- Scissors
- Photos or magazine pictures of different buildings
- White craft glue

1. Lay out the tarp to define the city limits. Help your child use the ruler and markers to draw streets, parks, and other desired features.

2. Trim magazine pictures of buildings to glue onto the face of your child's building blocks. A fun alternative is to help your child take photos of buildings in your neighborhood. Capture easy-to-recognize buildings such as city hall, the library, or the firehouse. Only a few blocks have to be decorated with pictures.

3. Let your child enjoy building a cityscape with the blocks.

Stuffed Blocks

Save money and add fun to your child's imaginative block play. These blocks are lighter than traditional wooden blocks as well.

Activity for an individual child

AGE GROUP: 18–40 months

DURATION OF ACTIVITY:
30 minutes

YOU WILL NEED:
- Newspaper
- Empty food boxes, such as those from cereal, rice, or macaroni and cheese
- Masking tape
- Decorative contact paper (optional)

1. Show your child how to crumple the newspaper into tight wads.

2. Have your child stuff the newspaper wads into the boxes. Be sure to stuff each box to the top.

3. Securely seal each box with tape.

4. If you wish, you can help your child decorate the blocks with contact paper.

Paper Logs

Here is a simple way to create safe logs for building and imaginative play.

Activity for an individual child

AGE GROUP: 18–40 months

DURATION OF ACTIVITY:
15 minutes

YOU WILL NEED:
- Newspaper
- Scotch tape

1. Spread three sheets of newspaper on the table.

2. Show your child how to roll the paper into tight tubes.

3. Securely seal each tube with tape.

4. Let your child make a lot of these to use for building, pretend campfires, and more.

Pretend Play Games

Most likely, your child will not need much encouragement to engage in pretend play on his own, but if he does, these activities can get the ball rolling. You will notice that each activity also promotes social interaction.

Act It Out

This simplified version of charades is a great activity for the whole family.

Activity for a group

AGE GROUP: 18–40 months

DURATION OF ACTIVITY:
20 minutes

YOU WILL NEED:
- White craft glue
- Magazine pictures of characters and animals that are easy to mime
- Index cards
- A hat or other container
- Kitchen timer

1. Before the game, glue the magazine pictures onto the index cards.

2. Place the cards into a hat or other container.

3. Each person gets a turn to "act it out." The player removes a picture from the hat and gets 10 seconds on the timer to imitate/mime the character on the card. When the time is up, other players guess the picture.

4. You can choose to let the person who guesses correctly have the next turn or the turns can be predetermined.

Animal Birthday Party

Tea parties are a well known make-believe activity. They are so much fun that your toddler won't even know that she is learning. All props are optional and can be replaced with your child's imagination!

Activity for an individual child or a group

AGE GROUP: 24–40 months

DURATION OF ACTIVITY:
15 minutes

YOU WILL NEED:
- A variety of stuffed animals
- Party hats (optional)
- Place settings (optional)
- Real or pretend food (optional)

1. Set all the animals around the table.

2. Encourage your child to pretend that someone is having a birthday.

3. Have her name the animals and decide who the birthday animal is.

4. Pretend to have the animals eat and sing "Happy Birthday."

Character in a Bag

This is a silly game that will get your child's imagination going! Be sure to use clothing that is easy to put on and take off.

Activity for a group

AGE GROUP: 18–40 months

DURATION OF ACTIVITY:
20 minutes

YOU WILL NEED:
- 3 paper grocery bags
- Markers
- A variety of clothing, shoes, and accessories (costume items add to the fun)

1. Label the bags with markers. You can number them or use shapes or colors to make it easier.

2. Sort the clothing, shoes, and accessories. Place the clothing in the first bag, the shoes in the second bag, and the accessories such as hats and handbags in the third bag.

3. Each person gets a turn to be a character. The player randomly pulls one item from each bag to put on. Once dressed, the person describes who he is and what he does.

Puppets

Puppets are magical. Not only can they breathe life into any story, but they often seem to have a wonderful effect on young children. Many children who are shy often feel more comfortable using puppets for expression. A child can project her own fears, wishes, and dreams through the character of a puppet. Make a puppet with your child and watch her imagination soar.

Rubber Finger Puppets

This is a quick and easy way to make finger puppet characters for your child.

Activity for an individual child

AGE GROUP: 30–40 months

DURATION OF ACTIVITY: 15 minutes

YOU WILL NEED:
- Scissors
- Old rubber dishwashing gloves
- Permanent markers

1. Cut the fingers off the rubber gloves.

2. Let your child use the markers to create a face and other features.

Bag Puppets

This is a traditional puppet craft. Frog puppets are especially cute to make.

Activity for an individual child

AGE GROUP: 18–40 months

DURATION OF ACTIVITY: 15 minutes

YOU WILL NEED:
- Small paper lunch bag
- Crayons or markers

1. Show your child how to insert her hand into the bag. Her thumb goes below the fold and her fingers go above it.

2. Encourage her to open and close her hand to make the puppet talk.

3. Let her decorate the puppet with crayons.

Sock Snakes

Your toddler will be able to create her own creative toy.

Activity for an individual child

AGE GROUP: 24–40 months

DURATION OF ACTIVITY:
15 minutes

YOU WILL NEED:
- Old tube socks
- Cotton balls or quilt stuffing
- Googly eyes
- Glue
- Markers

1. Help your toddler stuff a sock.

2. Tie off the end and use this end as the head.

3. Glue on googly eyes or use only markers to decorate if your toddler still puts things in her mouth.

4. If safe to do so, attach a ribbon that your toddler can use to pull the snake around.

5. Encourage your toddler to pretend the snake is navigating around the house or yard.

Big Head Puppets

This project takes a little more time and effort, but it is well worth it. Remember to use caution when using Styrofoam with young children because it can be a choking hazard.

Activity for an individual child

AGE GROUP: 18–40 months

DURATION OF ACTIVITY:
25 minutes

YOU WILL NEED:
- Scissors
- Styrofoam craft balls
- Markers
- White craft glue
- Yarn pieces
- Thin fabric remnants, 4"–5" square

1. Use the scissors to gouge a hole in the bottom of the Styrofoam ball. The hole should be wide enough to fit your child's finger and deep enough for her finger to fit in the ball to the first knuckle.

2. Let your child use the markers to decorate a face and other features.

3. Help her glue on the yarn pieces for hair.

4. When your child is ready to operate the puppet, have her drape the fabric over her index finger before attaching the head. The fabric becomes the puppet's body, and the middle finger and thumb become its arms.

Plate Puppets

Because this project is so simple, you may wish to let your child make a few puppets and then put on a show.

Activity for an individual child

AGE GROUP: 30–40 months

DURATION OF ACTIVITY: 15 minutes

YOU WILL NEED:
- Dessert-size paper plate
- Crayons
- White craft glue
- Wooden craft stick

1. Let your child decorate the plate with crayons to make a face.

2. Help her glue on the stick to use as a handle.

Walking Finger Puppets

You can make an endless cast of puppet characters this way.

Activity for an individual child

AGE GROUP: 18–40 months

DURATION OF ACTIVITY: 15 minutes

YOU WILL NEED:
- Scissors
- Cardboard or poster board
- Crayons or markers

1. Discuss with your child what characters he would like to make.

2. Cut out an outline of the character 4" tall. The outline should include the head, neck, arms, and torso, but not the legs.

3. Cut 2 holes ¼" from the edge of the bottom of the torso. These holes should be wide enough for your child's fingers to fit through and approximately 1" apart.

4. Let your child decorate the puppet with crayons or markers.

5. Have your child stick his fingers through the holes. Show him how to use his fingers for the puppet's legs and move them to make the puppet walk.

Chapter 9

The Best Games for Toddlers

Traditional Games

Many games have remained virtually unchanged as they have passed from generation to generation. You will also find similar variations in other cultures. Here are just a few classic games that your toddler might enjoy.

Hot and Cold

Help your child develop his listening skills and problem-solving abilities with this game.

Activity for an individual child

AGE GROUP: 30–40 months

DURATION OF ACTIVITY:
15 minutes

YOU WILL NEED:
- Small toy that can be easily hidden

1. When your child is out of the room, hide a small toy somewhere.

2. Have your child return to the room to look for the object. Guide him with verbal cues. When he is approaching the object, tell him, "You are getting hot." If he moves away from the object, tell him, "You are getting cold."

3. This game is most successful if you are expressive and emphatic in your responses. For example, as your child moves closer and closer to the hiding spot, you might say, "Ooh, you are getting warm. Okay, now you are hot. Wow! When you go by the couch, you are even hotter. Now you are burning up!"

Doggie, Doggie, Where's Your Bone?

Here is another game that is easy to adapt creatively with your child. You can change this game into, "Cupid, Cupid, Where's Your Heart?" or "Baker, Baker, Where's Your Cake?" or "Robin, Robin, Where's Your Worm?" Remember that young children may be uncomfortable closing their eyes, so don't worry about enforcing this.

Activity for a group

AGE GROUP: 30–40 months

DURATION OF ACTIVITY:
20 minutes

YOU WILL NEED:
• Small toy or dog bone

1. Have children sit cross-legged in a small circle on the floor. Be sure that there is plenty of room around them.

2. Choose one child to be "It." That child crouches in the center of the circle next to a toy or dog bone.

3. Tell the child who is "It" that he is the doggie and that he should pretend to nap by closing or hiding his eyes.

4. While "It" is pretending to nap, the rest of the players chant this rhyme:

DOGGIE, DOGGIE, WHERE'S YOUR BONE?
SOMEBODY TOOK IT AND RAN AWAY HOME.
WAKE UP, DOGGIE!

5. While the children are chanting, remove the bone and give it to one of the children to hide behind his back. All the children should pretend that they are also hiding the bone.

6. When the children say, "Wake up doggie," the child who is "It" rises and tries to guess who is hiding the bone.

7. The child with the bone becomes the new doggie.

Duck, Duck, Goose

The beauty of this traditional party game is that you can adapt it for any theme or occasion. Is it Easter? You can have the children play Bunny, Bunny, Chick. If they're learning about colors, the game can become Green, Green, Yellow.

Activity for a group

AGE GROUP: 30–40 months

DURATION OF ACTIVITY:
15 minutes

1. Have children sit cross-legged in a small circle on the floor. Be sure that there is plenty of room around them.

2. Choose one child to be "It." That child walks around the outside of the circle, gently tapping each child on the shoulder.

3. When "It" taps a child, he also calls out, "Duck." At a random point, "It" selects a child and calls out, "Goose!"

4. The goose must stand up and chase "It" around the circle.

5. "It" tries to run and sit in the vacant spot before the goose tags him. The goose then becomes the next person to be "It."

Cooperative Games

Many games that are played at elementary schools, playgrounds, and birthday parties encourage competition. This is not necessarily a bad thing. However, young toddlers have very diverse abilities, and they become easily frustrated when measured up against someone else. These cooperative games have the added benefit of helping young children learn positive social skills.

Keep It Up

You can adapt this activity according to the number of participants by simply adding more balls. You can also use balloons for this activity, but be vigilant with popped balloon pieces because they can be a choking hazard.

Activity for a group

AGE GROUP: 18–40 months

DURATION OF ACTIVITY:
15 minutes

YOU WILL NEED:
• 3 or 4 beach balls

1. To start the game, have participants stand in a circle.

2. Toss a few beach balls into the air. Have children imagine that they are bubbles or even fragile eggs.

3. The object is to bat, kick, or tip the balls to keep them from touching the ground.

4. When a ball hits the ground, it is removed from play. The game continues until all the balls are grounded.

Shrinking Island

This game can be played with children of all ages. It works best outdoors, as it requires a lot of space.

Activity for a group

AGE GROUP: 30–40 months

DURATION OF ACTIVITY:
15 minutes

YOU WILL NEED:
- Old blanket or sheet or several lengths of rope

1. You will need to define the boundaries of the island. You can use an old picnic blanket or sheet. Alternatively, you can set the boundaries with lengths of rope. Be sure that the area is large enough for all the players to comfortably stand.

2. Have participants circle around the island without stepping inside. You may wish to play music. Tell the players that they are swimming in the sea and have them imitate swimming motions as they circle around the island.

3. At the signal (music stops or verbal cue), the players must get out of the sea and go onto the dry land. Once everyone is safe, players can go back in the water.

4. After each round, the island becomes smaller and smaller. To make it shrink, fold the edges of the sheet under, or move the ropes closer together. The goal is for players to work together to make sure that everyone can fit on the island.

Octopus Tag

Also called hug tag, this is a less competitive version of regular tag.

Activity for a group

AGE GROUP: 30–40 months

DURATION OF ACTIVITY:
15 minutes

1. Like traditional tag, one person starts out being "It" and tries to tag other players.

2. When a player is caught, he joins arms with "It."

3. This ever-growing mass of children must stay connected and try to move as one to capture the next child.

Circle Chase

This game will help your child with eye-hand coordination and will also build her cooperation skills. Engage your child's imagination and add to the fun by assigning characters to the balls. Perhaps you can have the dog chase the cat or the bird chase the worm.

Activity for a group

AGE GROUP: 30–40 months

DURATION OF ACTIVITY:
10 minutes

YOU WILL NEED:
• 2 balls (must be different in size, color, or texture)

1. Have children sit cross-legged in a small circle on the floor.

2. Provide 2 balls for the children to pass. Like the game of Hot Potato, children pass objects around a circle. Do your best to have the children pass objects gently without throwing.

3. Tell the children this is a chasing game.

4. Each ball is a separate character in the chase. Start the balls at different places in the circle. Have children pass the balls until one "catches" the other.

What Could It Be?

This game will get everyone thinking outside of the box!

Activity for a group

AGE GROUP: 30–40 months

DURATION OF ACTIVITY:
20 minutes

YOU WILL NEED:
• A variety of common
  household objects

1. Hold up each object for children to see. Ask them to brainstorm possible nontraditional uses for it. Example: A spatula could be a lever or a fly swatter, and so on.

Sardines

This is a variation of Hide-and-Seek. This game usually results in lots of giggles. If a lot of children are playing or the hiding places are small, you can have more than one child hide.

Activity for a group

AGE GROUP: 30–40 months

DURATION OF ACTIVITY:
45 minutes

YOU WILL NEED:
• Kitchen timer (optional)

1. Designate one child to hide. Have the remaining children hide their eyes and wait. (You can have them count or you can use a kitchen timer.)

2. Once the waiting is over and the designated child is hiding, the hunt can begin.

3. When a seeker finds the hiding child, he quietly joins her in the hiding spot.

4. Each child who finds the hiders joins them. The children may have to squeeze together for all to fit (thus, the name of the game).

5. The last child to find the group becomes the next hider.

Games for Two

Here are some versatile activities that require very little setup and just two players. You can play these games with your child any time you have a few minutes or want to spend a little quality time with your toddler.

Shadow Tag

This game can be played with more than two, but it tends to get too chaotic. The game must be played outdoors in the morning or late afternoon when the shadows are long.

Activity for two players

AGE GROUP: 30–40 months

DURATION OF ACTIVITY:
15 minutes

1. This game is based upon the traditional game of tag. The difference is that the person who is "It" tries to tag the other person by stepping on his shadow. The other person dodges to protect his shadow. Remind players that this is not a contact sport.

Imagine That Hat

You can spark your toddler's imagination with just one simple prop.

Activity for two people

AGE GROUP: 30–40 months

DURATION OF ACTIVITY:
15 minutes

YOU WILL NEED:
- A variety of hats. Ones that suggest occupations or animals are best.

1. Place a hat on your toddler's head and have her act out the role the hat suggests. Take a turn yourself!

Mouth Music

Your young child loves to imitate, and this is a great way for him to learn!

Activity for two people

AGE GROUP: 18–30 months

DURATION OF ACTIVITY:
10 minutes

1. Lose your own inhibitions and demonstrate many sounds that you can make. Encourage your child to join in. Suggested actions include kissing the air, making raspberries with your tongue, humming, cooing, blowing through your lips, clicking your tongue, squeaking, and growling.

Paper Games

All you need is some creativity to make some cute activities for your toddler to enjoy. Your older child can also play more sophisticated paper games such as Tic-Tac-Toe or Hangman.

Halves

This is a cooperative activity. Older children may wish to try creating animals and other creatures, too. You can adapt this activity for three or four players by simply folding the paper into that many sections.

Activity for two people

AGE GROUP: 30–40 months

DURATION OF ACTIVITY:
15 minutes

YOU WILL NEED:
• 1 sheet white bond paper
• Crayons or markers for drawing

1. Fold the sheet of paper in half.

2. Each player draws half of a person on half of the paper, without seeing the other half.

3. One player draws a head, neck, and arms. Lines must extend a tiny bit below the fold so that the second player can see where to pick up.

4. The second player turns the paper over and draws the torso, legs, and feet.

5. Unfold the paper to reveal your work!

The Clown Says

This is a simple game that you can create that will help your child with following directions and motor development.

Activity for an individual child

AGE GROUP: 18–40 months

DURATION OF ACTIVITY:
10 minutes

YOU WILL NEED:
- Scissors
- Paper plate
- Poster board
- Brad (metal paper fastener, available at office supply stores)
- Markers

1. Make a small hole in the center of the paper plate.

2. Cut a small arrow out of the poster board, and make a small hole in the center. Use the brad to fasten the arrow to the plate. Leave it loose enough to spin freely.

3. Use the markers to draw a clown onto the plate; incorporate the spinner as one of his arms. (If your artistic skills are lacking, you can just call the game Stick Man Says.)

4. Divide the plate like a pie into 4 or 6 sections. In each section, either draw or glue on a picture that depicts a movement. For example, a picture of 2 hands could mean clapping.

5. Have your child spin the spinner, then act out the movement that the clown is pointing to. You may need to assist the younger child.

6. Consider taking a few turns yourself. Perhaps let your child spin the wheel for you.

Fast and Simple Games

There is no end to the games that you can create! The easiest place to start is to adapt some of the basic sports. A tennis ball and broom can be used for a golf game. Use a beach ball for a gentle variation of soccer. Here are some other ideas to get you started.

Bowling

Your child will be using his large motor skills when playing this game. You can set this game up inside or outside.

Activity for an individual child or a group

AGE GROUP: 18–40 months

DURATION OF ACTIVITY:
10 minutes

YOU WILL NEED:
• 6 clean 2-liter soda bottles
• 1 ball

1. Arrange the soda bottles like bowling pins. If you are playing outside, put some sand in the bottles to keep them from blowing over.

2. Show your child how to roll a ball to knock down the pins.

Wizard of Oz

This easy game is a variation of Peek-a-Boo.

Activity for an individual child

AGE GROUP: 12–24 months

DURATION OF ACTIVITY:
5 minutes

YOU WILL NEED:
• A stable curtain or drape

1. Show your child how to hide behind the drape or curtain. You can even have her go behind a shower curtain.

2. Either you or your child may push the curtain aside for the big reveal. Take turns hiding and revealing.

3. When you reveal, you may wish to make a funny face or posture to surprise your child. Then, ask your child to think of an imaginative way to surprise you on her next turn.

Chapter 10

Backyard and Nature Activities

Bugs!

You may be wrinkling your nose in disgust, but toddlers are naturally curious and usually only become afraid of insects when they are imitating the reactions of someone else. There are certainly more insects on this planet than any other species, and they are just about everywhere—so you might as well incorporate them into your child's creative play! This section includes some fun activities having to do with insects, but the most valuable activity may be to simply provide your child with a magnifying glass and some time to observe the insects all around him!

Catching Butterflies

This fun activity will help your child develop eye-hand coordination and motor skills.

Activity for an individual child

AGE GROUP: 18–40 months

DURATION OF ACTIVITY:
20 minutes

YOU WILL NEED:
- Scissors
- Construction paper in various colors
- Large kitchen strainer or aquarium net

1. Cut the construction paper into butterfly shapes. Be sure they are small enough to fit into your child's net.

2. Wait for a windy day. Go outside with your child. Toss one or more butterflies in the air and let your child try to catch them with the net.

Butterfly Feet

Your child will most likely enjoy the sensory experience of having his feet dipped in paint as much as he likes the end result.

Activity for an individual child

AGE GROUP: 18–40 months

DURATION OF ACTIVITY:
15 minutes

YOU WILL NEED:
- Shallow pie tin
- Washable tempera paint
- White poster board or construction paper
- Markers and crayons

1. Fill the pie tin with the paint. Help your child remove his shoes and socks, and then help him step into the paint.

2. Have him step directly out of the paint and onto the paper. Help him arrange his feet so he puts them down with heels together and toes pointed outward. (You can spread newspaper to catch any drips.) Have your child step directly off the paper again.

3. Once the picture is dry, your child can decorate the butterfly by drawing in a body and antennae.

Worm Tracks

This is a great open-ended art project for the child who finds these garden dwellers fascinating rather than icky.

Activity for an individual child

AGE GROUP: 18–40 months

DURATION OF ACTIVITY:
15 minutes

YOU WILL NEED:
- Brown tempera paint
- Shallow pie tin
- Yarn in different lengths and widths
- White construction or bond paper

1. Pour the paint into the pie tin.

2. Have your child dip and coat the yarn pieces in the brown paint.

3. Show her how to drag the yarn across the paper to create worm tracks.

Coffee-Filter Butterflies

Both adults and children will love these simple and colorful creations! You can also use colored tissue paper instead of dying the coffee filters.

Activity for an individual child

AGE GROUP: 18–40 months

DURATION OF ACTIVITY:
15 minutes

YOU WILL NEED:
- Disposable coffee filters
- Food coloring
- Wooden clothespins
- White craft glue
- Pipe cleaner, cut into 2"
  segments
- Markers

1. Open a coffee filter, and have your toddler squeeze different colored drops of food coloring onto it. The colors will blend together in a beautiful design.

2. Fold the colored filter into a fan shape and help your child insert it into the clothespin. Leave an equal amount of the filter on each side of the pin. Fluff out the coffee filter so that it looks like wings.

3. Let your child glue on the pipe cleaners to make antennae and use markers to make eyes on the head of the clothespin.

Fingerprint Bugs

These personalized insects will help your child develop creativity and fine motor skills.

Activity for an individual child

AGE GROUP: 18–40 months

DURATION OF ACTIVITY:
15 minutes

YOU WILL NEED:
• Washable tempera paint
• Pie tin
• White construction or bond paper
• Crayons

1. Pour the paint into the pie tin.

2. Have your child dip his thumb into the paint.

3. Help him press his thumb onto the paper to create a thumbprint. He can use crayons to add the head, legs, and antennae.

Cloud and Weather Activities

You do not have to go far to explore the world with your young child. The weather affects us all, and it is constantly changing. Regardless of your climate, there are many ways to explore and learn about weather. Here are some ideas for your budding scientist.

Cloud Watching

This classic activity is still one of the best ways to spend an afternoon. What a great way to spend some quiet and quality time with your young child while stimulating her imagination!

Activity for an individual child

AGE GROUP: 18–40 months

DURATION OF ACTIVITY:
30 minutes

1. Find a nice clear area where you and your child can lie down and watch the clouds. Be sure to encourage your toddler to use her imagination. Does she see animals, people, different shapes?

Cloud Blobs

You can bring the magic of cloud watching indoors with this simple and creative project.

Activity for an individual child

AGE GROUP: 18–40 months

DURATION OF ACTIVITY:
15 minutes

YOU WILL NEED:
- Dark-colored construction paper
- White tempera paint
- Small spoon
- Crayons

1. Instruct your child to use the spoon to place a small blob of white paint near the center of the paper.

2. Fold the paper neatly in half. Show your child how to gently rub the paper in all spots till there are no bulges.

3. Slowly unfold the paper. Have your child tell you what the blob looks like.

4. When the paint dries, your child may wish to embellish his creation with crayons.

Cloud Pictures

Your child will learn a bit about clouds and explore a unique texture with this project. Older toddlers can first color a landscape picture to use as a backdrop.

Activity for an individual child

AGE GROUP: 18–40 months

DURATION OF ACTIVITY:
15 minutes

YOU WILL NEED:
- Nonmenthol shaving cream
- White craft glue
- Thick paintbrushes
- Construction paper

1. Mix the shaving cream and glue in equal portions.

2. Have your child use this mixture as a paint to create cloud forms. The fluffy mixture will dry and become stiff.

Rain Painting

This is a great way for your child to observe how water reacts with other materials. Your child will also be able to experiment with mixing colors. This activity is only appropriate if your child will not be upset when the painting is altered.

Activity for an individual child

AGE GROUP: 18–40 months

DURATION OF ACTIVITY:
20 minutes

YOU WILL NEED:
- Food coloring
- Paper plate

1. Let your child create a colorful design by putting drops of food coloring onto a paper plate.

2. Have your child take her creation out in the rain to observe how the colors run when the rain falls on them. Be sure to stop before all the color is washed away or the plate becomes too soggy.

3. Return indoors, and let the altered picture dry.

Blown Pictures

This is a fun way for your child to learn about the power of an invisible force such as the wind and is a great venue for creative expression.

Activity for an individual child

AGE GROUP: 18–40 months

DURATION OF ACTIVITY:
10 minutes

YOU WILL NEED:
- Tempera paint
- Plastic spoons
- Light-colored construction or bond paper
- Plastic straws

1. Thin the tempera paint with water to the consistency of watercolor paint. Spoon small amounts of paint onto the paper.

2. Show your child how to use the straw to gently blow the paint around on the paper. You may need to poke a few small holes in the straw to prevent her from sucking instead of blowing the paint.

Blowing Games

Children enjoy seeing the cause and effect of their breath. Have them pretend that they are the north wind.

Activity for an individual child

AGE GROUP: 24–40 months

DURATION OF ACTIVITY:
15 minutes

YOU WILL NEED:
- Table or accessible flat surface
- Ping-Pong balls or cotton balls
- Straws (optional)

1. Set your child in front of a table or an accessible flat surface.

2. Place cotton balls or Ping-Pong balls near the edge of the surface.

3. Demonstrate how to blow the items across the surface. The child may use a straw or blow directly.

Outdoor Activities

Outdoors is often the best and healthiest place for your child to play and explore. When your child is outdoors, he is less restricted. He is free to use a louder voice, to move around more, and to make more of a mess.

Silly Walk

Take a normal, daily, routine activity and turn it into a fun opportunity to help your child develop balance and motor control.

Activity for an individual child

AGE GROUP: 18–40 months

DURATION OF ACTIVITY:
30 minutes

1. Challenge your toddler to take a silly walk with you. You can dictate the variations, or you may encourage your child to suggest ideas as well. Some silly steps that you can take on your silly walk may include walking on tiptoe or taking giant steps.

Picnic Ants

This game can be played indoors or outdoors and will help your child become more observant. You may wish to provide the participants with an old sheet and some fabric paints and let them decorate their own picnic blanket.

Activity for a group

AGE GROUP: 30–40 months

DURATION OF ACTIVITY:
15 minutes

YOU WILL NEED:
- 1 picnic blanket or sheet
- Assorted picnic items, such as thermos, paper plates, and napkins

1. Spread out the picnic blanket and arrange the picnic prop items in the center.

2. Have all the children close their eyes. Play the part of the pesky ant: Remove one item and hide it behind your back. (You may also choose one of the children to serve as the ant.)

3. Ask the children to open their eyes and guess which item was removed.

Magic Fairy Gardens

Your child's imagination will guide her in creating a mini garden perfect for fairies.

Activity for an individual child

AGE GROUP: 30–40 months

DURATION OF ACTIVITY:
20 minutes

1. Show your child how to use natural materials to create a mini garden in the yard. Moss can become grass; pebbles can become a wall; twigs serve well as fence posts. Your child will surely find more creative ideas!

Leaf Maze

Take advantage of all of those pesky leaves that have fallen on your lawn.

Activity for an individual child or a group

AGE GROUP: 18–40 months

DURATION OF ACTIVITY: 45 minutes

1. Before you rake up all of the fallen leaves in the autumn, clear thin paths through the leaves using a rake or a shovel. You can create a maze or a simple path to follow. If you are energetic, you can also do this with snow.

2. Tell children that they are squirrels that need to get through the path to find their acorns.

Paint Toss

This fun sensory activity encourages your child to be creative and expressive. This certainly gets messy, so be sure to put a smock or apron on your child or do it on a hot day when you can hose him off afterward!

Activity for an individual child

AGE GROUP: 18–40 months

DURATION OF ACTIVITY: 15 minutes

YOU WILL NEED:
- A large white sheet or butcher paper
- Tempera paint
- Pie tins
- Sponges or soft balls

1. Attach the sheet or paper onto a fence or the side of a garage.

2. Pour paint into pie tins.

3. Help your child dip the sponge into the paint and toss at the canvas.

Fun with the Hose

What a great way to cool off on a hot summer day! Like all water activities, adult supervision is needed at all times.

Activity for an individual child or a group

AGE GROUP: 18–40 months

DURATION OF ACTIVITY: 45 minutes

1. Take and keep control of the hose. Be sure not to spray any child who does not want to get wet, and try to avoid squirting anyone above the shoulders. Never allow anyone to squirt any child in the face or on the head, regardless of the child's age.

2. Option #1: Try a game of water limbo. Hold the hose so that the water sprays straight across, and challenge the children to duck under the spray without getting wet. Lower the water stream after everyone has had a turn.

3. Option #2: Hold the hose so water sprays in a long stream across the ground, and encourage players to jump over it. To increase the challenge, wiggle the hose.

Nature Crafts

People have been making creative crafts for thousands of years, long before glitter and crepe paper were available. They did without those items, and you can, too. There is no end to the amazing things that your toddler can create using natural materials. The best are those materials that your toddler has found on her own. Let the activities in this section inspire you to see things such as bark, seeds, and flowers in a whole new way.

Pinecone Bird Feeder

Not only will your toddler enjoy making this project, but the finished bird feeder will attract birds for your toddler to watch and enjoy!

Activity for an individual child

AGE GROUP: 18–40 months

DURATION OF ACTIVITY:
15 minutes

YOU WILL NEED:
- 12" length of yarn or twine
- 1 large pinecone
- 3 tablespoons smooth peanut butter
- 1 cup birdseed
- Shallow bowl or pie tin

1. Attach the yarn to the pinecone. Make a loop for hanging the bird feeder.

2. Help your toddler spread the peanut butter on the pinecone.

3. Pour the birdseed into the bowl. Show your child how to roll the pinecone in the seeds to coat it.

4. Take your bird feeder outside and hang it where your child will be able to watch the visiting birds.

Pressed Flower Collage

You will be surprised how easy it is to get a nice result from pressing flowers.

Activity for an individual child

AGE GROUP: 18–40 months

DURATION OF ACTIVITY: 3 days

YOU WILL NEED:
- Your choice of flowers
- Waxed paper or newspaper
- Wooden blocks or a large hardcover book

1. Arrange the blossoms between layers of newspaper or waxed paper. Press them under the wooden blocks or between the pages of a large book.

2. Have your child use the flowers to make a creative arrangement or collage.

Re-Stem a Flower

Here is another fun way to promote your child's creativity using flower petals.

Activity for an individual child

AGE GROUP: 24–40 months

DURATION OF ACTIVITY: 15 minutes

YOU WILL NEED:
- Contact paper
- A variety of flower petals (let your child help collect them)
- Green pipe cleaner
- Scissors

1. Cut two pieces of contact paper into a flower shape.

2. Have your toddler arrange the petals onto one piece. Lay pipe cleaner at the base for a stem.

3. Seal by pressing second sheet of contact paper on top.

Nature Collection

Here is a fun and easy way for your toddler to preserve all the treasures she picks up when she is exploring outside.

Activity for an individual child

AGE GROUP: 18–40 months

DURATION OF ACTIVITY:
30 minutes

YOU WILL NEED:
- Assortment of items that your toddler has found outside
- 1 sheet construction paper or poster board
- Clear contact paper

1. Help your child find and collect safe outdoor treasures. Good items include leaves, bark, twigs, and flowers. Watch out for small items that may pose a choking hazard if your toddler still puts things in her mouth.

2. Have your toddler arrange her treasures on the construction paper.

3. Cover the paper with clear contact paper. You will not have to glue anything and it will last a long time. (Alternatively, you can use a larger sheet of the contact paper. Have your child arrange her treasures on one half, and then fold the contact paper over to seal.)

Flower Crown

You can make this decorative craft project with your child at different times of the year to showcase the variety of natural materials and reflect the change in seasons.

Activity for an individual child

AGE GROUP: 18–40 months

DURATION OF ACTIVITY:
15 minutes

YOU WILL NEED:
- Paper plate
- Scissors
- Various flowers, seeds, grasses, and other natural materials
- White craft glue

1. Fold the paper plate in half. Cut out a semicircle, leaving a 3" border. Cut spikes and square shapes to a depth of 1".

2. Open the plate. The spikes and squares become the spires of the crown.

3. Have your child collect a variety of natural materials to glue on the crown for decoration.

4. Let the glue dry before helping your child don the crown.

Magic Sun Prints

This activity seems to work like magic. This is a fun way to explore the sun's power as well as shadows and shapes.

Activity for an individual child

AGE GROUP: 18–40 months

DURATION OF ACTIVITY:
3–4 hours

YOU WILL NEED:
- A variety of objects with different shapes
- Dark-colored construction paper

1. Ask your child to help you find objects to use to make silhouettes. Flat objects work best. Some good examples include keys, erasers, forks, and shoelaces.

2. Go outside on a sunny day. Have your toddler arrange the chosen objects on the dark construction paper.

3. Leave the paper out in full sunlight for a few hours. The sun will fade the exposed paper to a lighter shade than the paper protected by the selected objects.

4. Remove the objects to reveal the silhouette designs.

Astronomy and Nighttime Activities

Nighttime can mean more than bedtime for your child. Darkness still provides plenty of interesting activities and things to do and learn. Take your child out on a clear night and introduce him to the wonder and mystery of the night sky in a way that makes him feel safe. Your child will enjoy watching the phases of the moon and, if you're lucky, maybe you will spot a shooting star!

Binoculars

Although these "binoculars" do not work, you may find that they encourage your child to be observant and interested in the night sky. Because rubber bands can be a choking hazard, be sure to supervise your child when making this craft and playing with the finished product.

Activity for an individual child

AGE GROUP: 18–40 months

DURATION OF ACTIVITY:
20 minutes

YOU WILL NEED:
- 4 large rubber bands
- 2 squares clear plastic wrap
  or tinted cellophane
- 2 toilet paper tubes
- Crayons
- Star-shaped stickers
  (optional)

1. Use a rubber band to secure a square of plastic wrap or cellophane over 1 end of each toilet paper tube.

2. Attach the 2 rolls together side by side with the remaining rubber bands.

3. Give your child crayons and stickers to decorate the binoculars.

4. Go outside on a clear night, and use the binoculars to look at the moon and the stars. If you have real binoculars or a telescope, be sure to bring that along, too.

Dot to Dot

The original constellations and astrological signs that we know came from someone's imagination.

Activity for an individual child

AGE GROUP: 18–40 months

DURATION OF ACTIVITY:
15 minutes

YOU WILL NEED:
- Dark-colored paper with random white spots (you can prepare this in advance or have your child make it)
- White chalk

1. Show your child a constellation chart and point out some of the simpler forms.

2. Encourage your child to connect the dots to create a shape or character. Ask her to give her new constellation a name.

Starry Starry Night

Encourage your child to be creative when creating his own picture of the night sky.

Activity for an individual child

AGE GROUP: 24–40 months

DURATION OF ACTIVITY:
15 minutes

YOU WILL NEED:
- Dark-colored construction paper
- Star- and moon-shaped sponges or cookie cutters
- Pie tins
- Yellow and white tempera paint

1. Pour paint into tins.

2. Show your toddler how to dip the sponge or cookie cutter and then press onto the paper to create a print.

Chapter 11

Building Literacy

Skills and Readiness

Before your child is ready to learn letter identification and phonics, there are many other skills that you can focus on. For a child to be ready to learn to read, she needs to develop auditory memory and auditory discrimination as well as visual memory and discrimination. Memory is recalling and recognizing sounds or images. Discrimination is the ability to distinguish the difference in sounds or images. Your child also needs to learn the symbolic nature of written language—in other words, that words are talk written down. Additionally, building your child's vocabulary will help her with reading later on.

Captions

This is a great introduction to creative storytelling and is a fantastic way to show your child that words are talk written down. Your child will be particularly motivated to "read" her own words.

Activity for an individual child

AGE GROUP: 30–40 months

DURATION OF ACTIVITY:
10 minutes

YOU WILL NEED:
- Crayons or markers
- Bond paper
- Picture book (optional)

1. Whenever your child draws or paints a picture, ask her to tell you about what she created. Write down her words, and create a caption for the artwork. Be sure to read it back to her.

2. As an alternative, you can show your child photos or pictures in a book. Invite her to supply a caption by asking her to tell a story about the picture. Again, be sure to write down and review her words.

What Did You Say?

Enhance your child's listening skills and auditory discrimination with this silly activity.

Activity for an individual child

AGE GROUP: 30–40 months

DURATION OF ACTIVITY:
15 minutes

1. Review a picture book or magazine with your child.

2. As you are browsing the pictures, point to different objects and identify them. Ask your child to listen closely.

3. On occasion, intentionally misidentify a picture. For example, point to a picture of a car and say "can," or point to a picture of a boat and say "goat."

4. Have your child stop you when she catches you making a mistake. Ask her to say the word correctly.

Who Said That?

This fun game will help your child with auditory memory skills. You can also play this game using sounds from common household objects that make distinctive noises, such as an alarm clock or telephone.

Activity for an individual child

AGE GROUP: 18–40 months

DURATION OF ACTIVITY:
15 minutes

YOU WILL NEED:
- White craft glue
- Photos or magazine pictures of animals
- Index cards
- Recording of animal sounds that match the pictures

1. Glue the pictures to the index cards.

2. Play the recording of animal sounds. Ask your child to hold up the picture showing the animal that makes that sound.

Using Books

A love for books and reading is a gift that will last your child a lifetime. Remember, books are not decorations to be gazed at from afar. If you are worried that your toddler will rip or chew a book, buy him books that are made to be extra durable. Let your child have the opportunity to look at books and peruse the pictures. These activities are a great way to use books as a springboard for further literacy development.

Creative Re-enactment

This activity will help your child with story comprehension, memory, and creativity. A simpler variation of this activity is to have your child act out specified motions that are mentioned in the story. For example, you might ask your child, "Can you huff and puff like the big bad wolf?"

Activity for an individual child

AGE GROUP: 18–40 months

DURATION OF ACTIVITY: 15 minutes

1. Review a well-known and beloved picture book or story with your child.

2. As you slowly read or recite the tale, have your child act out the drama.

A New Story

Engage your child's imagination and build his vocabulary with this activity. It is interesting to see the differences between your child's story and the original.

Activity for an individual child

AGE GROUP: 30–40 months

DURATION OF ACTIVITY: 15 minutes

YOU WILL NEED:
• 1 new picture book

1. Present a new picture book to your child, and ask him to examine the pictures.

2. Ask him to guess and describe what is happening in the story. For younger children, each picture will have its own tale. You can help your older child link the sequences of the pictures together for a more involved story.

3. If you wish, you can extend this activity by asking your child to draw his own picture to supplement his story. Perhaps his picture can depict what he thinks will happen next.

Storytelling

Long before the invention of the printing press, fables, myths, and tales were being shared with young children. Each time the tale was told, it was shaped by the teller's interpretation and expression. Even if you have dozens of wonderful children's books in your home, put down the books and spin a yarn for your young child once in a while. You have the opportunity to bring a story to life. Use different voices and facial expressions to add interest. Encouraging children to make up stories is a great way to facilitate imagination as well as promote both early verbal and written literacy skills. Get started by involving children as you develop a tale.

Going on a Bear Hunt

Young children will love the suspense you can create as you engage their imagination. You can modify this for any animal you wish.

Activity for an individual child or a group

AGE GROUP: 24–40 months

DURATION OF ACTIVITY: 15 minutes

YOU WILL NEED:
- 7–15 paper cutouts in the shape of animal footprints

1. Lay out the footprints to create a path for your toddler to follow. You can adjust the complexity and length of the path according to your toddler's ability.

2. Teach your toddler the following chant and prompt her to repeat each line:

GOING ON A BEAR [OR OTHER ANIMAL] HUNT,
GOING TO CATCH A BIG ONE.
READY? LET'S GO!

3. Quietly follow the path as you hunt the bear or other animal.

4. Encourage your child to add to the chant and the story. Other lines in the chant could be: "Going to look under a tree," "Going to look behind this rock," and so on.

5. Ask your child what she imagines would happen if she found the animal she is looking for.

Story in a Bag

Here is a way you can spark your child's creativity and encourage her to create her own stories.

Activity for an individual child

AGE GROUP: 30–40 months

DURATION OF ACTIVITY:
15 minutes

YOU WILL NEED:
- 5 or 6 common objects
- 1 paper bag

1. Place 5 or 6 common objects into a paper bag. Suggested items include keys, a bell, a comb, and a flower.

2. Have your child remove the items from the bag. You can either have your child look at all of the items at once, or have her remove the objects one at a time. Help her create a story incorporating these items. For example, "One day a man heard a bell ring. He combed his hair. He used his keys to lock his door, and he took a flower to his friend."

3. Consider having your child draw illustrations for her story. Alternatively, write down her story so that you can reread it together.

Fill-in Story

This is a silly activity, like the school-age game of Mad Libs. Each story will be unique.

Activity for an individual child

AGE GROUP: 18–40 months

DURATION OF ACTIVITY:
15 minutes

YOU WILL NEED:
- White craft glue
- Magazine pictures of animals and objects
- Index cards

1. Glue the pictures to the index cards, and place them in a hat.

2. Recite a well-known nursery rhyme or fairy tale. Stop at points in the story where a substitution can be made. Ask your child to pull a card from the hat.

3. Substitute the new word into the story for a silly result. For example, "Little Red Riding Hood was taking a basket to her grandmother. Her mom reminded her to take flowers with her also" might become, "Little Red Riding Hood was taking a rake to her grandmother. Her mom reminded her to take kittens with her also."

Next Line, Please

This is a game that can be played by all members in your family. This a great activity for long plane rides or when you have to wait somewhere.

Activity for an individual child or a group

AGE GROUP: 30–40 months

DURATION OF ACTIVITY: 15 minutes

1. Each person takes a turn by adding a sentence to the evolving story. No one player can have control over what will happen, but the adult may need to keep the story somewhat on track.

2. Your new story may evolve like this:

PARENT: ONE DAY THERE WAS A BEAR WHO . . .

CHILD: LIVED IN A HOUSE.

PARENT: THIS BEAR WAS HUNGRY AND . . .

CHILD: THE BOY LIKES TOYS.

PARENT: SO THEY GOT TOGETHER TO GET LUNCH AND GO TO THE TOY STORE. WHEN THEY GOT THERE THEY SAW . . .

3. Once again, consider having your child draw illustrations for her story. Alternatively, write down her story so that you can reread it together.

Verbal Games

You can engage your toddler in verbal games in just about any place at any time. These games promote his vocabulary development, expressive language skills, auditory memory, auditory discrimination, and listening skills. Young children are often very fond of these activities as they feature interaction with you!

Rhyme Time

This activity will help your child with auditory discrimination skills and build her vocabulary.

Activity for an individual child

AGE GROUP: 30–40 months

DURATION OF ACTIVITY:
15 minutes

YOU WILL NEED:
- White craft glue
- Magazine pictures of animals and objects
- Index cards

1. Glue the pictures to the index cards.

2. Show your child a card, and have her identify the picture.

3. Ask her to generate rhymes for the picture. Not all rhymes have to be real words. For example, if the picture is of a cat, potential rhymes could include bat, fat, gat, lat, and mat.

Play Phone

What better way to get your child talking and build vocabulary than to have him use the phone?

Activity for an individual child

AGE GROUP: 18–40 months

DURATION OF ACTIVITY:
15 minutes

YOU WILL NEED:
- Toy phone (or unplugged real one)

1. Encourage your child to pretend to call a friend or loved one. Your child will probably not need much encouragement. Don't be surprised if he carries on full conversations, imagining the other person's part.

Flannel-Board Activities

Discover what many preschool teachers already know: flannel boards are a great way to engage young children in a story. You can make the story more concrete and involve the child directly. You may choose to buy a readymade felt board kit, or you can make one yourself with some felt scraps and Velcro.

Story Board

Here is a fun way to bring a story to life. You can also use nursery rhymes and simple poems with this activity.

Activity for an individual child

AGE GROUP: 30–40 months

DURATION OF ACTIVITY:
15 minutes

YOU WILL NEED:
- Scissors
- Felt
- Flannel board
- White craft glue

1. Choose a well-known, simple story to illustrate.

2. Cut out felt pieces in the shapes of the main characters and props. For the story "The Three Billy Goats Gruff," you would need three goats, a troll, and a bridge.

3. Recite the story, and have your child glue the pieces onto the flannel board to match the action of the tale.

Outline Match

Your toddler will have fun while learning about shapes and developing skills in visual discrimination and problem solving.

Activity for an individual child

AGE GROUP: 30–40 months

DURATION OF ACTIVITY:
15 minutes

YOU WILL NEED:
- Scissors
- Felt
- Flannel or felt board
- White chalk

1. Cut out a variety of shapes and figures from the felt.

2. Place the pieces on the flannel board and outline them with the chalk.

3. Trim the shapes to make them slightly smaller than the outlines.

4. Challenge your child to fit the pieces inside the outlines.

DIY Book Activities

What better way to help your child develop a love of books than to have her create a book of her own? You can bet your child will be more motivated to read when she is reading her own words. As your child grows, you may wish to continue this practice. Books can become more involved and may feature ABCs or something of special interest to the child, such as family pets or hobbies. This activity will also help your child understand the symbolic use of words.

Book Covers

If a picture is worth a thousand words, a book cover should tell a tale all on its own . . .

Activity for an individual child

AGE GROUP: 30–40 months

DURATION OF ACTIVITY:
15 minutes

YOU WILL NEED:
- Paper bag or white contact paper
- Crayons or markers

1. Create a book cover with the paper bag or contact paper. Put it on one of your toddler's favorite books.

2. Have your toddler decorate the book cover. Encourage him to creatively depict the story inside.

Scrapbook

Scrapbooking is a very popular hobby. Why not let your toddler create a scrapbook of her own?

Activity for an individual child

AGE GROUP: 30–40 months

DURATION OF ACTIVITY:
15 minutes

YOU WILL NEED:
- Photographs
- Mementos and souvenirs
- Scrapbook/photo album
- Scissors
- Index cards
- Markers

1. Let your child select the photos and mementos she wants to include in her scrapbook.

2. Cut the index cards into strips to use as labels.

3. Encourage your child to dictate a label or even a short commentary for each item in the book. Attach the label to the scrapbook.

Chapter 12
All about Me

Learning-about-Family Activities

Your child's first relationships are with her family. By learning about families in general and about her family specifically, your toddler will learn how people interact with, love, and support each other. She will also learn her role in your family. You will notice that some of the activities in this chapter involve other family members. This is a great way to build family cohesion with your toddler as she learns.

I Know Your Nose

Can your child identify other family members by just looking at a nose or other facial feature? This activity develops visual discrimination and problem-solving skills.

Activity for an individual child

AGE GROUP: 18–40 months

DURATION OF ACTIVITY:
15 minutes

YOU WILL NEED:
- Scissors
- Close-up portraits of family members, including one of your toddler
- White craft glue
- Index cards

1. Cut out each family member's facial features (eyes, nose, and mouth).

2. Glue all of the eye sets to one index card, all of the noses on another, and the mouths on a third.

3. For each card, challenge your toddler to identify the owner of the facial feature.

4. To extend this activity, omit the step of gluing the pictures onto the index cards; instead, tape them on temporarily. Let your child remove them and create a new person by jumbling the facial features into a new face.

Gingerbread Family

Your child will enjoy being creative while he represents his family in a unique way. Remember you can also do this with real gingerbread dough and then bake the finished project.

Activity for an individual child

AGE GROUP: 30–40 months

DURATION OF ACTIVITY:
15 minutes

YOU WILL NEED:
- Brown construction paper or cardstock
- People-shaped cookie cutters
- Skim milk
- Small bowls
- Food coloring
- Paint brushes
- Jimmies or sprinkles

1. Help your child trace around the cookie cutters to create a template on the paper.

2. Help your child cut out the shapes. Make different sizes for different family members.

3. Mix the food coloring into the skim milk.

4. Have your child paint his family cookies to decorate them, just like he would with icing.

5. Let him sprinkle the jimmies on top of the icing for a finishing effect.

Learning-about-My-Body Activities

From the moment your child discovered his own toes, he has been learning about his body and how it works. Toddlers are often eager to learn about the body and will show pride and share their knowledge as they explore and identify their body parts.

All about Me

Your toddler will delight in seeing a life-size copy of himself. If you cannot get a large enough roll of paper, you can use an old sheet and fabric paints instead.

Activity for an individual child

AGE GROUP: 18–40 months

DURATION OF ACTIVITY:
15 minutes

YOU WILL NEED:
- Large roll of butcher paper
- Markers
- Crayons

1. Have your child lie flat on his back on the paper. Experiment with different positions of his arms and legs. Trace an outline around his body.

2. Point out to your child the different body parts on the outline. Label them if you wish.

3. Let your child color the outline with crayons.

Face Paint

Easy to apply, easy to wash off. Now your child can pretend to be a clown for the day! If you are bold, let your child make you into a fantasy character too!

Activity for an individual child

AGE GROUP: 18–40 months

DURATION OF ACTIVITY:
10 minutes

YOU WILL NEED:
- 1 part cornstarch
- ½ part water
- ½ part cold cream
- Food coloring

1. Mix all the ingredients together and apply with cotton swabs.

Build a Person

Your child develops his fine motor skills, creativity, and problem-solving ability as he pieces together a person.

Activity for an individual child

AGE GROUP: 18–40 months

DURATION OF ACTIVITY:
30 minutes

YOU WILL NEED:
- Body shapes cut from construction paper, or magazine pictures of body parts
- White craft glue
- 1 piece of poster board

1. If you are using construction paper pieces, be sure to keep them very simple, such as a torso, arms, legs, and head. If you use magazine pictures, consider involving your child in the search for appropriate clippings.

2. Assist your child in gluing the body-part pieces to the poster board to create a person.

I Am Special

As your toddler grows, she develops a self-concept. She is becoming increasingly aware that she is an individual person with her own tastes, interests, and personality. Early on, she will have experiences that shape her self-concept and esteem. Both directly and indirectly, she will be receiving messages about her worth and competence. You can plan specific activities that will reinforce the message that she is indeed very special.

Self-Portrait

Have your toddler create a self-portrait a few times a year. This is a great way to measure her progress in self-image as well as motor control.

Activity for an individual child

AGE GROUP: 18–40 months

DURATION OF ACTIVITY:
15 minutes

YOU WILL NEED:
- Light-colored construction or bond paper
- Crayons
- White craft glue (optional)
- Yarn and fabric scraps (optional)

1. Provide your child with paper and crayons to create a self-portrait.

2. If desired, let her glue on yarn for hair and scraps of fabric for clothes.

All-about-Me Collage

Here is a great chance for your child to build self-expression and self-esteem! He'll also get to showcase his interests and favorite items.

Activity for an individual child

AGE GROUP: 36–40 months

DURATION OF ACTIVITY:
15 minutes

YOU WILL NEED:
- Old magazines
- Scissors
- Glue
- Construction paper

1. Have your child find magazine pictures that express who he is and what he likes. Examples include favorite foods or games he likes to play.

2. Help your child cut out the pictures that he chooses.

3. Have him glue the pictures onto the paper.

All-about-Me Book

Your child can create a lasting memory. She will enjoy "reading" it as much as she did creating it. You can bind the pages together with a stapler or by punching holes in the sides and attaching the pages with a yarn bow.

Activity for an individual child

AGE GROUP: 18–40 months

DURATION OF ACTIVITY:
45 minutes

YOU WILL NEED:
- Markers
- Light-colored construction or bond paper
- Magazines
- Scissors
- White craft glue

1. Label each page of your child's book with a title, such as "My Favorite Foods" or "Toys I Play With."

2. Help your child find appropriate pictures in the magazines to cut out and paste onto the pages.

Where Would I Go?

Let your child imagine his next vacation! His creativity should lead the way—his trip could be to the next town over or halfway across the world.

Activity for an individual child

AGE GROUP: 30–40 months

DURATION OF ACTIVITY:
20 minutes

YOU WILL NEED:
- Construction paper
- Scissors
- Markers or crayons
- Old magazines (optional)
- Glue (optional)

1. Help your child cut out a suitcase shape from the construction paper. Ask him where he would go on his trip, how he would get there, and what he would pack. Have him decorate the suitcase to depict his answers.

2. If you have extra time, help your child cut out images from the magazines that show where he chose to go or what he chose to pack and paste them on the suitcase shape.

Monkey in the Mirror

Young children are often fascinated by mirrors and their own images. Your toddler may enjoy simply making silly faces in the mirror. Don't worry—the dry-erase ink is easy to remove with glass cleaner and a paper towel.

Activity for an individual child

AGE GROUP: 30–40 months

DURATION OF ACTIVITY:
10 minutes

YOU WILL NEED:
- Mirror
- Dry-erase markers

1. Have your child stand in front of the mirror and show her how she can use the markers to trace over her image. She may also want to give herself a hat or other accessories.

Paint a Song

This activity will help your child with emotional expression and creativity. Let him choose his favorite music to start, but then encourage him to listen to new types as well.

Activity for an individual child

AGE GROUP: 18–40 months

DURATION OF ACTIVITY: 15 minutes

YOU WILL NEED:
- Large sheet of poster board
- Tempera paint
- Pie tins
- Paintbrushes
- Variety of music recordings

1. Set up the paper and paints for your child to create.

2. Play music of differing tempos and moods. Ask your child to listen to the music and let the music guide the way he paints. For example, when listening to a waltz, he could paint with slow, sweeping strokes.

Learning to Be Safe and Healthy

It is never too early to teach your child about keeping healthy. Although you can do activities with him, remember that your child will learn by your example. If you want your child to make good food choices, be mindful of what you eat. If you want your child to brush his teeth, be sure to brush yours as well.

Paper-Plate Meals

Help your child learn about nutrition and balanced meals with this activity. You may wish to introduce the concept of the basic food groups here.

Activity for an individual child

AGE GROUP: 30–40 months

DURATION OF ACTIVITY:
30 minutes

YOU WILL NEED:
- Magazines
- Scissors
- White craft glue
- Paper plates

1. Go through the magazines with your child and help him select food pictures that he wants to include in his "meal."

2. Assist your child in tearing or cutting out the selected pictures.

3. Show your child how to glue the food onto the plate to create a meal. You could create a separate plate for each meal of the day.

Feed Me!

Here is a fun way to help your child start to make healthy food choices.

Activity for an individual child

AGE GROUP: 30–40 months

DURATION OF ACTIVITY:
45 minutes

YOU WILL NEED:
- Scissors
- 1 large sheet poster board or cardboard
- Markers and crayons
- Food pictures cut from magazines

1. Cut a large head (approximately the size of a beach ball) out of poster board. Cut out a hole for the mouth.

2. Have your child help you decorate the head.

3. Provide your child with a variety of magazine clippings of food pictures. Be sure to have a wide selection of both nutritious and junk foods. Ask your child to feed the head with only those foods that are nutritious.

Sparkle Germs

Young children are often resistant to washing their hands. It is hard for them to understand things that they cannot see. Here is a concrete way to teach them about germs and the importance of washing hands.

Activity for an individual child

AGE GROUP: 30–40 months

DURATION OF ACTIVITY:
10 minutes

YOU WILL NEED:
- Craft glitter

1. Sprinkle a bit of glitter onto your child's hands. Explain that these glitter specks are like germs, which can make him sick. The germs are very small and they stick to you and get passed along.

2. Have your child touch different surfaces and shake hands with other people. Show him how the germs (glitter) spread.

3. Have your child wash his hands and see how the germs are washed away.

Brush the Tooth

It is never too early to teach your child about the importance of good dental hygiene.

Activity for an individual child

AGE GROUP: 18–40 months

DURATION OF ACTIVITY:
10 minutes

YOU WILL NEED:
- Scissors
- 1 sheet yellow construction paper
- An old toothbrush
- White tempera paint

1. Cut a tooth shape from the construction paper.

2. Talk with your child about teeth and how when they are not brushed, they can develop decay and turn yellow.

3. Let him use the toothbrush to paint the tooth with pretend toothpaste (white paint).

Chapter 13
Favorite Toddler Themes

Animal Activities

Many young children are fascinated by animals. Your child may enjoy watching videos of animals on television as well as seeing them at the zoo. Your child may begin her exploration of animals at home, with the family pet. Here are some activities for learning about more exotic animals.

Animal Safari

Engage your child's imagination as you take her on a pretend safari. You may wish to add ambience by playing a recording of jungle sounds in the background.

Activity for an individual child

AGE GROUP: 18–40 months

DURATION OF ACTIVITY:
10 minutes

YOU WILL NEED:
• Assorted stuffed animals

1. When your child is out of the room, hide a variety of stuffed animals.

2. Have your child return and search for the "wild" animals. Encourage her to name the animals that she finds.

Animal Reunion

Your toddler will learn more about animals as well as develop problem-solving skills with this activity.

Activity for an individual child

AGE GROUP: 30–40 months

DURATION OF ACTIVITY:
30 minutes

YOU WILL NEED:
- Pictures of animals
- White craft glue
- Index cards

1. Enlist your child's help in finding pictures of animals as adults and as babies. Old *National Geographic* magazines are a great source for animal pictures.

2. Glue one animal picture to each index card.

3. Have your child match up the babies with their parents.

Crawling Critters

Your toddler can pretend to be any number of critters that crawl.

Activity for an individual child

AGE GROUP: 18–40 months

DURATION OF ACTIVITY:
15 minutes

YOU WILL NEED:
- Pillows

1. Arrange pillows in piles and spread some out.

2. Encourage your toddler to crawl over the pillows, pretending to be a creature that crawls, such as a lizard, raccoon, or anything she can imagine.

Stuffed Snake

Here is a cute craft for your child. When she is done, she will have a new stuffed animal to play with.

Activity for an individual child

AGE GROUP: 18–40 months

DURATION OF ACTIVITY:
15 minutes

YOU WILL NEED:
- 1 knee-high nylon stocking
- Cotton fiber fill or wadded-up newspaper
- Scissors
- Felt pieces
- White craft glue

1. Help your child stuff the stocking with the cotton or newspaper. Leave a few inches empty at the end, and tie a secure knot for the tail.

2. Cut out eyes and a mouth from the felt pieces. Let your child attach the features with glue. If your child is still putting things in her mouth, consider using a permanent marker to draw on facial features instead.

Monkey See, Monkey Do

Like toddlers, monkeys are known for their ability and desire to imitate. Here is a silly game that you can play with your child. This is basically a version of Follow the Leader. Consider reading the book *Caps for Sale*, by Esphyr Slobodkina, before you play this game.

Activity for an individual child or a group

AGE GROUP: 18–40 months

DURATION OF ACTIVITY:
10 minutes

1. The lead monkey performs different silly movements and dances that the other players must imitate. Take turns so everyone has a chance to be the lead monkey.

Dog Biscuits

Your child will have a blast making homemade treats for her dog.

Activity for an individual child or a group

AGE GROUP: 18–40 months

DURATION OF ACTIVITY: 45 minutes

YOU WILL NEED:
- ½ cup cornmeal
- 6 tablespoons oil
- ⅔ cup water or meat broth
- 2 cups whole wheat flour

1. Stir all ingredients together. If dough seems a bit dry, add a few drops of water. If dough seems too wet, add more flour a little at a time.

2. Turn the dough out onto a floured surface. Show your child how to knead the dough.

3. Help her roll the dough out to ¼" thick. Let her cut out the biscuits with cookie cutters—a bone shape would be best.

4. Place biscuits on a cookie sheet and bake at 350°F for 30 minutes or until biscuits are light brown.

Handprint Sheep

Engage your child's senses with this personalized craft.

Activity for an individual child or a group

AGE GROUP: 18–40 months

DURATION OF ACTIVITY: 15 minutes

YOU WILL NEED:
- Construction paper
- Pencil
- White craft glue
- Cotton balls
- Crayons

1. Have your child put her hand, palm down, onto a piece of construction paper. Have her spread her fingers.

2. Use the pencil to trace around her hand. Turn the shape upside down; the four fingers become legs and the thumb is the head.

3. Show your child how to glue the cotton balls to create a fleecy effect.

4. Let her color in the feet and the face with crayons.

Community Helpers

At a very early age, children start to imitate adults. Your child may want to put on Mom's shoes or Dad's tie and pretend to be a grownup. He will start to show an interest in the roles that adults play. In addition to trying these activities with your child, consider making field trips to watch these community helpers in action.

You've Got Mail

This is a fun pretend activity that will also build language skills. You can extend this idea by exchanging real mail with someone like a grandparent!

Activity for an individual child

AGE GROUP: 30–40 months

DURATION OF ACTIVITY:
15 minutes

YOU WILL NEED:
- 2 shoeboxes
- Scissors
- Paint
- Postcards
- Crayons
- Used stamps
- Glue stick

1. Place the lids on the boxes and cut a hole in each large enough for a postcard to fit.

2. Have your child paint the boxes as he wishes. Designate one for you and one for him.

3. Show your child how to create a postcard by writing or drawing a message. Help him affix the used stamp with the glue stick.

4. Have him place the postcard in your box.

5. Engage your child in a pretend game of sending mail back and forth to each other.

Firefighters

Many young children like to make-believe that they are rescue helpers and heroes. It helps develop their self-esteem and gives them a much-needed sense of power. You can add to the fantasy with further props and outfits.

Activity for an individual child

AGE GROUP: 30–40 months

DURATION OF ACTIVITY:
15 minutes

YOU WILL NEED:
- Red, orange, and yellow chalk
- A garden hose
- Empty buckets

1. In advance, go outside and draw chalk "flames" in different areas on the ground or on buildings.

2. Encourage your toddler to use the hose and/or buckets to douse the fire by washing away the chalk illustrations.

Many Hats

Many professionals can be identified by the hats they wear. Here is a guessing game based on this concept.

Activity for an individual child

AGE GROUP: 18–40 months

DURATION OF ACTIVITY:
15 minutes

YOU WILL NEED:
- White craft glue
- Pictures of different hats
- Index cards

1. Glue the pictures on the cards. Ask your child to look at each card and guess who wears that hat. (Suggested hats include a chef's hat, baseball cap, firefighter hat, police motorcycle helmet, nurse's cap, and hard hat.)

Transportation

Transportation is a fun theme to explore with your child. Because young children learn best through direct, hands-on experience, take your child for a ride on different forms of transportation when you can. Perhaps your city still has a streetcar or trolley system. If you live in a rural area, can you go for a hayride on a local farm?

Rolling

Many forms of transportation move on wheels. Consider taking your child somewhere she can see the tracks that wheels leave in the mud or snow.

Activity for an individual child

AGE GROUP: 18–40 months

DURATION OF ACTIVITY:
15 minutes

YOU WILL NEED:
- Small toy cars and trucks
- Washable dark-colored tempera paint
- Shallow pie tin
- Light-colored construction paper

1. Show your child how to gently dip the wheels of the vehicles into the paint after you've poured it into the tin.

2. Let her create interesting patterns and designs by rolling the vehicles back and forth across the paper.

3. Be sure to wash the toys off when you are done.

Ship Scoot

Your child's imagination can take him further than any ship could sail. You will find this to be a popular activity even for older children.

Activity for an individual child

AGE GROUP: 24–40 months

DURATION OF ACTIVITY:
15 minutes

YOU WILL NEED:
- A blanket or small area rug
- Props, such as treasure chest, toy fish, etc. (optional)

1. Place the rug in the middle of a hardwood or tile floor. Have your toddler sit with knees bent and feet flat on the floor in the middle of the rug.

2. Show him how to scoot by extending and bending his legs. He can also paddle by pushing off with his arms.

3. The floor area can become a wide ocean to explore!

Toy Airplane

Much simpler than a real model, you and your toddler can construct this airplane. Be aware that the plane will be too heavy and fragile to fly, but that probably won't stop your toddler from trying it out anyway!

Activity for an individual child

AGE GROUP: 18–40 months

DURATION OF ACTIVITY:
20 minutes

YOU WILL NEED:
- Scissors
- Paper towel tube
- Poster board
- Paper cup
- Tissue paper scraps

1. Cut a 1" slit through both sides of the paper towel roll.

2. From the poster board, cut two wings. Make each the size and shape of an adult's index finger. Make sure that the wings will fit into the slots.

3. Cut tiny slits up from the rim of the paper cup. This is to slightly widen the top of the cup, which will become the cockpit.

4. Help your child slide the wings in the slits and place the cup over one opening of the tube. You may need to secure the cup with some glue.

5. Provide your child with tissue paper scraps to glue on for decoration.

My Car

Engage your child's imagination with this project. Your child can also build a boat, train, airplane—whatever her imagination and creativity dictates.

Activity for an individual child or a group

AGE GROUP: 18–40 months

DURATION OF ACTIVITY: 30 minutes

YOU WILL NEED:

- Scissors
- Large box (an appliance box works well)
- Markers or tempera paint
- Stapler (optional)
- Foil pie tins (optional)

1. Let your child decide where she would like you to cut windows or doors in the box.

2. Let your child decorate her vehicle however she wishes.

3. If you wish, you can staple on the pie tins for wheels.

The Wheels on the Bus

Try adapting this song to sing about other forms of transportation. You can easily sing about the sails on the boat or the propeller on the plane.

Activity for an individual child

AGE GROUP: 18–40 months

DURATION OF ACTIVITY: 10 minutes

1. Sing or chant the following with your child. Encourage her to use appropriate motions:

THE WHEELS ON THE BUS GO ROUND AND ROUND, ROUND AND ROUND, ROUND AND ROUND.
THE WHEELS ON THE BUS GO ROUND AND ROUND, ALL THROUGH THE TOWN.

(ROLL HANDS)

2. Other verses:

THE WIPERS ON THE BUS GO SWISH, SWISH, SWISH.
THE DOOR ON THE BUS GOES OPEN AND SHUT.
THE SEATS ON THE BUS GO BUMP, BUMP, BUMP.

Dinosaurs

Although dinosaurs are long gone, they still capture the interest and imagination of young children. Many toddlers love to learn about these gigantic creatures from the past.

Dinosaur Egg

Your child will be delighted to crack open the egg to find a dinosaur. Be sure to involve him in making the egg, too. You should closely supervise this activity. Because both the toy and the balloon can be choking hazards, this activity is best for children who no longer put things in their mouths.

Activity for an individual child

AGE GROUP: 30–40 months

DURATION OF ACTIVITY:
30 minutes plus 1 day for project to dry

YOU WILL NEED:
- 1 balloon
- Small plastic dinosaur toy
- Papier-Mâché
- Tempera paint

1. Slightly inflate the balloon and insert the toy. Completely inflate the balloon and tie.

2. Coat the balloon with Papier-Mâché (see Chapter 5). Once the Papier-Mâché is dry, your child can paint the egg.

3. Ask your child how long he thinks the egg should sit in a "nest" before he cracks it open (until the next meal, until morning, etc.).

Digging for Bones

Here are two fun ways to show your child how dinosaur fossils were found. To extend this activity, let your child glue the bones together to create his own creature.

Activity for an individual child

AGE GROUP: 18–40 months

DURATION OF ACTIVITY:
10 minutes

YOU WILL NEED:
• Smooth chicken bones, or Popsicle sticks
• Sandbox

1. Start with smooth chicken bones. Be sure there are no sharp or splintered pieces. Boil and thoroughly clean the bones. You could add a drop of bleach to the boiling water to make them look older.

2. Bury the bones in the sandbox for your child to find.

The Ocean

You do not have to live near the shore to introduce your child to all the fascinating things under the sea. You can find some great props and artifacts such as shells and coral to share with your child.

Paper Bag Whale

Your child may wish to make a group of these—if so, she can have a pod of whales.

Activity for an individual child

AGE GROUP: 18–40 months

DURATION OF ACTIVITY:
15 minutes

YOU WILL NEED:
• Brown paper bag
• Newspaper
• String
• Gray and black tempera paint

1. Have your child stuff the bag with crumpled-up newspapers. Be sure that she leaves a little room near the opening.

2. Draw the bag closed and tie. Leave a little paper past the knot to serve as the tail.

3. Let your child paint her whale any way she wants.

Margarine-Tub Jellyfish

You can create this cute little sea creature in a flash. If you want to have your child play with the jellyfish in the water, substitute yarn for the crepe-paper tentacles, and coat the tissue-paper-and-felt body with clear fingernail polish.

Activity for an individual child

AGE GROUP: 18–40 months

DURATION OF ACTIVITY:
15 minutes

YOU WILL NEED:
- White craft glue
- Tissue paper
- Margarine tub
- Lengths of crepe paper, ribbon, or yarn
- 2 felt circles

1. Have your child glue tissue paper onto the margarine tub.

2. Once the body is dry, your child can glue on the crepe-paper tentacles and the felt eyes.

Deep-Sea Dive

This activity will engage your child's imagination and expand her vocabulary as she learns more about the ocean and aquatic life. For added excitement, let your child wear a snorkel mask.

Activity for an individual child

AGE GROUP: 18–40 months

DURATION OF ACTIVITY:
15 minutes

YOU WILL NEED:
- Blanket
- Deep-sea items such as sea sponges, shells, starfish, toy sea animals, and pieces of coral

1. Drape a sheet or blanket over a table. Blue is best, but any color is okay.

2. Place a variety of deep-sea items under the table. Suggested items include sea sponges, shells, starfish, toy sea animals, and pieces of coral.

3. Have your child "dive" under the sheet (sea) and bring back a treasure. Ask her to identify what she found.

Birds

Birds are interesting for kids to watch since they move around frequently, sing pretty songs, and are easy to find!

Bird's Nest

If you have the chance, show your child a real-life bird's nest. Talk about what he would use to build a nest if he were a bird. When this nest is complete, your child might want to put a toy bird or eggs in it.

Activity for an individual child

AGE GROUP: 18–40 months

DURATION OF ACTIVITY:
20 minutes

YOU WILL NEED:
- Heavy-duty poster board
- Mud
- Leaves and grass
- Sticks, twigs, and pine needles

1. With the poster board as a base, let your child make a mixture of the mud and the leaves and grass.

2. Help him form the mixture into a nest shape.

3. Let him add the sticks, twigs, and pine needles for interest.

Feed the Baby Bird

Here is a fun way to promote bonding while having fun pretending that you and your child are birds.

Activity for an individual child

AGE GROUP: 30–40 months

DURATION OF ACTIVITY:
15 minutes

YOU WILL NEED:
- A brown blanket or cover
- Gummy worms, candy, strips of bell peppers, or green beans

1. Have your toddler curl up in the brown blanket and pretend to be the baby bird in a nest.

2. Flap your arms as you approach him.

3. Pretend to be the mother bird as you feed him a gummy worm. Be sure he chews it well.

Eggshell Scramble

Your child can explore eggshells while making a creative art project.

Activity for an individual child

AGE GROUP: 24–40 months

DURATION OF ACTIVITY:
15 minutes

YOU WILL NEED:
- Construction paper (cut into the shape of an egg if you wish)
- Eggshells

1. Break up eggshells and set aside to dry. You may wish to dye them or leave them their natural color.

2. Encourage your toddler to glue the shells onto the paper in a creative design.

Bird in the Cage

Your child will love finding the bird in the cage. You might help your child make his own bird out of clay to use for this craft. Remember to collect and dispose of broken balloon pieces, which can be a choking hazard.

Activity for an individual child

AGE GROUP: 30–40 months

DURATION OF ACTIVITY:
1 hour

YOU WILL NEED:
- Small toy bird, bought or homemade
- Balloon
- Water
- White craft glue
- Small bowl
- Yarn or twine

1. Help your child insert the bird into the balloon.

2. Inflate and tie the balloon.

3. Mix the water and glue in a bowl to form a thick liquid. Show your child how to dip pieces of yarn into the glue mixture. Have him let the excess glue drip off and then wrap the yarn around the balloon. Encourage him to cover about 75 percent of the balloon.

4. When the glue is dry, pop the balloon. What will remain is the bird in the cage.

Pond Life

Exploring pond life is a great way to learn more about nature and the environment. You can introduce your child to the concept of life cycles by observing frogs. You can begin a discussion about habitats, where different animals live, and what they eat, too.

Lily-Pond Hop

Here is a cute way to teach your child a little bit about frogs and help develop her large motor skills as well. If your child is not yet coordinated enough to jump, help her leap or take a big step.

Activity for an individual child

AGE GROUP: 18–40 months

DURATION OF ACTIVITY:
15 minutes

YOU WILL NEED:
• Carpet squares or mats

1. Set up carpet squares or mats in a pattern around the room. Be sure that they are placed close enough together for your child to jump from one to another.

2. Talk about how frogs live in ponds and jump from lily pad to lily pad. Show your child how to jump like a frog.

Turtle in a Shell

With just one simple prop you can launch your child's imagination. If you have time, you and your child can also create a more elaborate shell using a box.

Activity for an individual child

AGE GROUP: 24–40 months

DURATION OF ACTIVITY:
15 minutes

YOU WILL NEED:
• Large blanket or furniture throw

1. Demonstrate to your toddler how to crawl with the blanket over her back.

2. Have her keep her head and limbs out.

3. Encourage her to pretend that she is a turtle looking for food. Ask her to hide in her shell when she is frightened.

Frog's Dinner

This fun game will help your child learn more about frogs while she develops coordination as well. You can get small plastic insects from a dollar store or a bait-and-tackle shop.

Activity for an individual child

AGE GROUP: 18–40 months

DURATION OF ACTIVITY:
15 minutes

YOU WILL NEED:
- White craft glue
- Velcro discs
- Small plastic flies and insects
- Paper party blowers

1. Glue Velcro to each insect.

2. Attach Velcro to the end of the party blower.

3. Show your child how to blow the paper party favor so that it unrolls. Show her how to use this as a frog's tongue to catch the bugs.

Fairy Tales

Young children enjoy the classic fairy tales and rhymes. By sharing the stories and these activities, you will be helping your child develop literacy skills and imagination!

Sail Away

For a change, let your child drag a favorite toy or teddy bear around.

Activity for an individual child

AGE GROUP: 18–36 months

DURATION OF ACTIVITY:
10 minutes

YOU WILL NEED:
- Towel or blanket

1. Have your child sit or lay in the center of an old towel or blanket. If possible, do this on a hardwood or linoleum floor.

2. Slowly drag your child around and point out imaginary points of interest. Example: While passing the couch you can say, "Look, there goes the king's castle!"

Crowns

A crown is a great prop for promoting imaginative play.

Activity for an individual child

AGE GROUP: 24–40 months

DURATION OF ACTIVITY:
15 minutes

YOU WILL NEED:
- Strip of cardstock paper
- Scissors
- Tinfoil
- Tape
- Glitter glue

1. Cut points on the strip of paper into a zig-zag to create the crown. Tape the strip into a circle that fits your toddler's head.

2. Show your toddler how to wrap the crown in tinfoil.

3. Let your child embellish the crown with glitter glue.

Which Is the Best?

You may wish to start this activity by reading the story of Goldilocks and the Three Bears first.

Activity for an individual child

AGE GROUP: 24–40 months

DURATION OF ACTIVITY:
20 minutes

YOU WILL NEED:
- 3 bowls of oatmeal with spoons (one very warm, one cold, and one just the way the child likes it)
- 3 chairs or pillows (one with a board under it to make it stiff, one very soft, and one just the way the child likes it)
- 3 sweaters (one too small, one too big, and one just the child's size)

1. Tell your child that not everyone is suited for the same things.

2. Present the oatmeal, call it porridge, and ask your child to pick the one he would want.

3. Repeat with the cushions and the shirts. This time, let your child try them out if he wants.

Cinderella's Shoe

Bring the Cinderella story to life and promote problem-solving skills at the same time.

Activity for an individual child

AGE GROUP: 24–36 months

DURATION OF ACTIVITY:
10 minutes

YOU WILL NEED:
- 1 fancy shoe or slipper
- Kitchen timer, (optional)

1. Read the story of Cinderella to your child.

2. Hide the chosen shoe. Turn on the kitchen timer and have your child find the shoe before "midnight."

Giant Shoes

What young child would pass up an activity that encourages him to be loud and rambunctious? Because your child won't be able to move as nimbly as usual, you need to closely supervise this activity.

Activity for an individual child

AGE GROUP: 30–40 months

DURATION OF ACTIVITY:
15 minutes

YOU WILL NEED:
- Scissors
- 2 shoeboxes
- Masking tape
- Recording of marching music

1. Cut a hole in the center of each shoebox lid just big enough to fit your child's foot.

2. Securely tape the lids to the boxes.

3. Help your child insert his feet into the boxes.

4. Once he is able to walk in his shoebox shoes, play some marching music and encourage him to march and stomp in time with the music.

Chapter 14

Preschool Concepts Made Fun

Shapes

When your child is learning about shapes, he is learning about basic mathematical and spatial concepts. Start to broaden your child's awareness by pointing out the shapes of everyday objects.

Shape Hunt

As your child searches for shapes, he is also developing visual discrimination skills that will help him with reading when he is older.

Activity for an individual child

AGE GROUP: 18–40 months

DURATION OF ACTIVITY: 15 minutes

YOU WILL NEED:
- Construction paper
- Scissors
- Butterfly net

1. From the construction paper, cut out a circle, a square, and a triangle.

2. Work with one shape at a time. Show your child the shape, and tell him that he is going on a shape hunt. Help him find other items that are that shape. For example, show him the circle and then go around the room looking for circles. Help him find circles in things like a doorknob, a plate, or a clock, and briefly capture them in the net before you move on.

Shape Characters

These cute characters and rhymes will help your child with shape identification.

Activity for an individual child

AGE GROUP: 18–40 months

DURATION OF ACTIVITY:
15 minutes

YOU WILL NEED:
- Construction paper
- Scissors
- Crayons

1. From the construction paper, cut out a circle, a square, and a triangle. Let your child color in facial features for each shape.

2. Teach your child the following rhymes for each shape:

I AM SUZY CIRCLE, WATCH ME BEND
ROUND AND ROUND FROM END TO END.

TOMMY TRIANGLE IS THE NAME FOR ME;
COUNT MY SIDES: ONE, TWO, THREE.

SAMMY SQUARE IS MY NAME;
MY FOUR SIDES ARE ALL THE SAME.

Shape Collage

In addition to learning about a shape, your toddler will have an opportunity for creative expression.

Activity for an individual child

AGE GROUP: 30–40 months
(beyond the age that she will put things in her mouth)

DURATION OF ACTIVITY:
15 minutes

YOU WILL NEED:
- Construction paper
- Small items of chosen shape
- Glue or school paste

1. Let your toddler glue items of a certain shape onto the paper. Triangular items may include an office clip, a magnet, a bent pipe cleaner, or an arrow. Square items could include a Scrabble tile, an eraser, or a stamp. Circular items could include a lid, cereal, a rubber band, or a ring. Encourage her to make a creative collage!

Circle Prints

Let your child use his creativity while he explores the circle shape.

Activity for an individual child

AGE GROUP: 18–40 months

DURATION OF ACTIVITY:
20 minutes

YOU WILL NEED:
- Tempera paint
- Pie tin
- Circular objects
- Construction paper

1. Pour some paint into the pie tin.

2. Have your child help you find circular items to use. Try jar lids or the rim of a paper cup.

3. Show your child how to dip items in the paint and then press them onto the paper to create circle prints.

Does Not Belong

This activity teaches visual discrimination in the same way as the well-known Sesame Street song, "One of These Things Is Not Like the Other." You can make many game pieces in varying degrees of complication.

Activity for an individual child

AGE GROUP: 30–40 months

DURATION OF ACTIVITY:
15 minutes

YOU WILL NEED:
- Ruler
- Light-colored construction or bond paper
- Markers or crayons

1. Using the ruler, draw lines to divide each sheet of paper into 4 equal sections.

2. Draw or color identical shapes or pictures in 3 of the sections. Choose a different square on each sheet to leave blank.

3. Draw an item that is different from the others in the fourth square. For example, you may have 3 squares and 1 triangle, 3 red dots and 1 blue dot, or 3 dogs and 1 cat.

4. Ask your child to identify the object that is different.

Shape Animals

This activity will help your child use problem-solving skills as well as help him with shape identification.

Activity for an individual child

AGE GROUP: 30–40 months

DURATION OF ACTIVITY:
20 minutes

YOU WILL NEED:
- Scissors
- Construction paper
- White craft glue
- 1 sheet poster board

1. Precut a variety of shapes from the construction paper, making multiples of each shape as well as different sizes of each.

2. Show your toddler how to arrange the shapes to create the forms of animals. For example, a triangle could be the head, and four circles can be used for paws. Glue each animal to the poster board.

3. Help your child identify the shapes that he uses. Encourage your child to talk about the animal that he made. Did he make a lion, a bear, or perhaps a new species altogether?

Colors

There are many activities that can help your child learn color identification. The most successful activities are hands-on, spark his imagination, and engage his senses. Here are just a few to get you started.

Rainbow Discs

Here is a way for your child to see the world through many-colored lenses. This activity can also serve as an introductory lesson on mixing colors.

Activity for an individual child

AGE GROUP: 18–40 months

DURATION OF ACTIVITY:
20 minutes

YOU WILL NEED:
- 6 paper plates
- Scissors
- Red, yellow, and blue cellophane
- White craft glue

1. Put two paper plates together and cut a hole in the center about the size of a plum.

2. Cut a piece of colored cellophane slightly larger than the hole.

3. Glue the cellophane to the top of one plate to cover the hole.

4. Set the second plate on top of the first and help your child glue them together. Now you have a rainbow disc for your child to look through.

5. Repeat these steps to make two more discs in the remaining colors. Show your child how to overlap the discs to create new colors.

Fishing for Colors

This fun game will help your child develop her eye-hand coordination while learning to identify colors. You need to closely supervise this activity at all times—the "fishing line" could wrap around your child, and the magnets and clips could pose a choking hazard.

Activity for an individual child

AGE GROUP: 30–40 months

DURATION OF ACTIVITY:
20 minutes

YOU WILL NEED:
- 1 piece of string 2' long
- 1 smooth stick or dowel rod
- 1 small magnet
- Scissors
- Colored construction paper
- Paper clips

1. Tie the string around the end of the stick and then attach the magnet to serve as the hook.

2. Cut the construction paper into fish shapes several inches in length.

3. Attach a paper clip to the head of each fish.

4. You can place the fish on the floor or put them in an empty aquarium.

5. Show your child how to use the magnetized fishing pole to "catch" a fish. Have her identify the color of the fish she catches.

Numbers

Children develop a mathematical awareness at an early age. Although your toddler is not ready for mathematical equations, you can start to introduce him to the concepts of quantity and the symbolic representation of quantity.

Birthday Cake

Here is a fun way to help your child see the relationship between numerals and quantity.

Activity for an individual child

AGE GROUP: 30–40 months

DURATION OF ACTIVITY:
15 minutes

YOU WILL NEED:
• Scissors
• Construction paper
• Markers
• White craft glue

1. Cut the construction paper in the shape of a cake. Repeat to make 5 cakes.

2. Mark the assigned number on the side of the cake.

3. Cut out 15 thin rectangle shapes for candles. Cut out tiny yellow teardrop shapes for flames and glue them onto the candles.

4. For each cake, help your child identify the number and glue on the appropriate number of candles.

Three Little Kittens

Use this popular rhyme to reinforce number concepts with your toddler. You can also do this activity with "The Three Bears" and their bowls of porridge.

Activity for an individual child

AGE GROUP: 30–40 months

DURATION OF ACTIVITY:
10 minutes

YOU WILL NEED:
- 3 photos of different cats
- 6 mittens (or paper cutouts of mittens)

1. Recite the following rhyme for your toddler:

THREE LITTLE KITTENS,
THEY LOST THEIR MITTENS,
AND THEY BEGAN TO CRY,
OH, MOTHER DEAR,
WE SADLY FEAR
OUR MITTENS WE HAVE LOST.
WHAT! LOST YOUR MITTENS,
YOU NAUGHTY KITTENS!
THEN YOU SHALL HAVE NO PIE.
MEE-OW, MEE-OW, MEE-OW, MEE-OW.
YOU SHALL HAVE NO PIE.
THE THREE LITTLE KITTENS,
THEY FOUND THEIR MITTENS,
AND THEY BEGAN TO CRY,
OH, MOTHER DEAR,
SEE HERE, SEE HERE,
OUR MITTENS WE HAVE FOUND.
WHAT! FOUND YOUR MITTENS,
YOU DARLING KITTENS!
THEN YOU SHALL HAVE SOME PIE.
MEE-OW, MEE-OW, MEE-OW, MEE-OW.
YOU SHALL HAVE SOME PIE.

2. Set up the three pictures and have your child count and distribute the mittens for each cat.

Letters

Your young child is just starting to learn to decode and interpret symbols. Although you may consider letter recognition an important skill, be sure to keep the learning activities fun! Letter recognition is only one step in developing literacy skills and will not be fully mastered for a few years yet.

Letter Collages

Here is a concrete way to help your toddler with letter identification and the sounds the letters make. Close supervision is needed when you are working with small objects.

Activity for an individual child

AGE GROUP: 30–40 months

DURATION OF ACTIVITY: 30 minutes

YOU WILL NEED:
- Scissors
- Poster board
- White craft glue
- Variety of small objects

1. Cut your chosen letters from the poster board. Make them 8"–10" high, leaving plenty of room to glue objects.

2. Help your child select and then glue appropriate objects onto the letter. For example, glue buttons on the "B" or glue pennies on the "P."

Homemade Clay

This clay dries nicely. Note: The thicker the sculpture, the longer it takes to dry.

Activity for an individual child

Makes 3 cups

AGE GROUP: 18–40 months

DURATION OF ACTIVITY: 30 minutes

YOU WILL NEED:
- 2 cups baking soda
- 1 cup cornstarch
- 1¼ cups cold water

1. Mix all the ingredients together and cook over a medium heat while stirring constantly.

2. When mixture reaches the consistency of mashed potatoes, remove from the heat and place on a clean counter or plate. Cover the clay with a damp cloth until it is cool.

3. Knead the clay, then mold and sculpt as desired into letters. Let your child paint the dried letters.

Spatial Concepts

Helping your child learn spatial concepts will help her master mathematical and reading skills when she enters school. These activities will also help her to learn to follow directions and build her vocabulary.

Hey Diddle Diddle

Use the famous nursery rhyme to help your child learn spatial concepts.

Activity for a group

AGE GROUP: 30–40 months

DURATION OF ACTIVITY:
15 minutes

YOU WILL NEED:
- Masking tape
- Cutout or photograph of the moon
- 1 sheet poster board
- Cutout or photograph of a cow

1. Tape the moon onto the poster board. Stick a loop of tape to the back of the cow.

2. Teach your child the classic nursery rhyme "Hey Diddle Diddle." Ask your child questions like, "Did you ever see a cow jump over the moon?" or "Do you think a cow can really jump that high?"

3. Ask your child to stick the cow "over" the moon.

4. Introduce variations to the rhyme and have your child place the cow in the appropriate place each time. Examples: the cow hid under the moon, the cow danced beside the moon, and so on.

The Noble Duke of York

This is a traditional action song that will get your child moving while she learns directions. Be sure to act out the part of a general.

Activity for an individual child

AGE GROUP: 18–40 months

DURATION OF ACTIVITY: 15 minutes

1. Teach your child the following song and the movements that accompany it:

THE NOBLE DUKE OF YORK,
HE HAD 10,000 MEN.

(HOLD UP TEN FINGERS)

HE MARCHED THEM ALL STRAIGHT UP A HILL

(POINT UP AND RISE UP ON TIPTOES)

AND MARCHED THEM DOWN AGAIN.

(POINT DOWN AND SQUAT TO THE GROUND)

AND WHEN THEY'RE UP, THEY'RE UP UP UP!

(POINT UP AND RISE UP ON TIPTOES)

AND WHEN THEY'RE DOWN, THEY'RE DOWN, DOWN, DOWN!

(POINT DOWN AND SQUAT TO THE GROUND)

AND WHEN THEY'RE ONLY HALFWAY UP,

(STOOP HALFWAY)

THEY'RE NEITHER
UP NOR DOWN!

(QUICKLY JUMP UP AND THEN LAND ON THE GROUND)

Chapter 15

Seasonal Activities

Fall

Harvest time is a fun season to celebrate with your child. Take this opportunity to talk about where food comes from. If you can, consider a trip to a local commercial farm. Many have programs for children where they can pick their own pumpkins, taste fresh apple cider, or participate in other activities.

Apple Prints

Celebrate harvest time with a bounty of fresh apples. This activity will help your child have fun with this popular fruit.

Activity for an individual child

AGE GROUP: 18–40 months

DURATION OF ACTIVITY:
10 minutes

YOU WILL NEED:
- Knife
- 1 apple
- Paper towel
- Tempera paint
- Shallow pie tin
- Light-colored construction paper

1. Cut the apple in half crosswise. Dry off the inside with a paper towel.

2. Pour a small amount of paint into the pie tin.

3. Show your toddler how to grasp the apple to dip it into the paint. Have her press the painted apple on the paper to create a print. The effect will look a little like a star.

Squirrel It Away

This is a fun game that will help your child engage in fantasy and learn about squirrels at the same time.

Activity for an individual child

AGE GROUP: 24–40 months (beyond the age that she will put things in her mouth)

DURATION OF ACTIVITY: 15 minutes

YOU WILL NEED:
- Acorns, walnuts, or pecans in the shell

1. In advance, hide the nuts around the yard.

2. Teach your toddler the following rhyme:

GREY SQUIRREL, GREY SQUIRREL, SWISH YOUR BUSHY TAIL
GREY SQUIRREL, GREY SQUIRREL, SWISH YOUR BUSHY TAIL
WRINKLE UP YOUR LITTLE NOSE
PUT A NUT BETWEEN YOUR TOES
GREY SQUIRREL, GREY SQUIRREL, SWISH YOUR BUSHY TAIL

3. Encourage your child to pretend to be a squirrel and go find the nuts.

Homemade Pumpkin

If your child is too small to carve a pumpkin or doesn't like the feel of the seeds and stringy flesh, try making this paper-bag version!

Activity for an individual child

AGE GROUP: 18–40 months

DURATION OF ACTIVITY: 15 minutes

YOU WILL NEED:
- Brown paper bag
- Old newspapers
- Small piece of ribbon
- Orange tempera paint
- Markers

1. Have your child fill the paper bag ⅔ of the way with crumpled-up pieces of newspaper. Tie the top of the bag with the ribbon, leaving a little bit of bag for the "stem."

2. Have her paint the bag with the orange paint. When it's dry, she can add a face or her own decorations with the markers.

Cornucopia

What is a more popular symbol of harvest than the cornucopia (horn of plenty)? Here is an easy way to make one. While you are working on this project, take the time to discuss with your child where different foods come from.

Activity for an individual child

AGE GROUP: 30–40 months

DURATION OF ACTIVITY:
20 minutes

YOU WILL NEED:
• 1 sheet brown construction paper
• Masking tape
• Magazines
• Scissors

1. Roll the sheet of brown paper to create a horn shape. Secure the edges with tape.

2. Go through the magazines with your child to find appropriate items to add to the cornucopia. Explain that the cornucopia holds food from a harvest: fruits and vegetables that have been picked.

3. Assist your child in cutting out the magazine pictures or have her tear out the pictures. Let her tape the food into the cornucopia.

Corn Rolling

This simple painting activity produces a unique effect. You may also wish to have your toddler try painting and printing with other vegetables, such as potatoes, cauliflower, and green peppers.

Activity for an individual child

AGE GROUP: 18–40 months

DURATION OF ACTIVITY:
15 minutes

YOU WILL NEED:
• 1 dried ear of corn
• Tempera paint
• Shallow pie tin
• Light-colored construction paper

1. Have your child roll the corncob in the paint in the tin the same way that you would a paint roller.

2. Your child can then roll out different patterns and designs on the paper.

Harvest Bowling

Help develop your child's motor skills while exposing her to some fall vegetables. Your child will enjoy exploring the different colors and interesting textures. Look for gourds that are shaped like bottles, with a wide base and thin neck.

Activity for an individual child or a group

AGE GROUP: 30–40 months

DURATION OF ACTIVITY:
20 minutes

YOU WILL NEED:
- 5 small dried gourds
- Masking tape
- 1 or 2 small round pumpkins

1. Set the gourds up like bowling pins.

2. Stick a strip of masking tape to the floor to make a start line. This should be quite close to the gourds, as the pumpkins will not roll very far.

3. Show your child how to roll the pumpkins to knock down the gourds. Don't worry about keeping score.

Leaf Rubbings

This is a great way for your child to explore the different shapes and textures of autumn leaves. Avoid leaves that are already dried out.

Activity for an individual child

AGE GROUP: 30–40 months

DURATION OF ACTIVITY:
10 minutes

YOU WILL NEED:
- A variety of autumn leaves that your child has collected
- Light-colored bond paper
- Peeled crayons

1. Have your child place one leaf or a group of leaves under the sheet of paper.

2. Show your child how to use the side of a crayon to rub on the paper. The shape and texture of the leaf will be revealed.

Leaf Crown

Your child will enjoy making this crown. He can use it as a prop in his imaginative play.

Activity for an individual child

AGE GROUP: 18–40 months

DURATION OF ACTIVITY:
10 minutes

YOU WILL NEED:
- Scissors
- 2 sheets construction paper
- Stapler
- White craft glue
- A variety of autumn leaves

1. Cut a strip or strips of construction paper and staple them together to make a band that will fit your child's head.

2. Help your child glue the leaves to his crown.

Leaf Glitter

Here is a new way to add pizzazz to your child's drawing and artwork. You may choose to add store-bought glitter to the mix.

Activity for an individual child or a group

AGE GROUP: 18–40 months

DURATION OF ACTIVITY:
20 minutes

YOU WILL NEED:
- Colorful autumn leaves, slightly dry
- White craft glue
- Construction paper

1. Help the child crumble up the leaves into fine pieces.

2. Let your child sprinkle leaf "glitter" onto his glue design on the paper. He may also choose to add the leaf glitter to other pictures he has made.

Winter

When you wake up to find that it has snowed overnight, you may be annoyed or even angry. To you, snow means shoveling, hazardous roads, and longer commutes. To your child, however, snow is a magical wonderland! Take the time to remember the fun of playing in the snow.

Paper Bag Penguin Puppet

Celebrate this cold-weather species with an extra-cute puppet!

Activity for an individual child

AGE GROUP: 24–40 months

DURATION OF ACTIVITY: 20 minutes

YOU WILL NEED:
- Brown paper bag
- Orange, white, and black construction paper
- Glue
- Markers
- Googly eyes, if your child is old enough not to put things in his mouth

1. First, have your child cut out some shapes (or help him do so): a white circle the same size as the bottom of the bag (for the face), a large white oval the same size as the length of the bag (for the body), orange strips for "hair," an orange triangle (for the beak), and 2 black triangles (for the penguin's feet).

2. Paste the face onto the bottom of the bag. Show your child how to put his hand inside the bag so he can envision how the puppet will work. Paste or draw on the rest of the penguin's face (hair, eyes, and beak).

3. Tuck part of the black triangle "feet" behind the body and paste them in place. Then glue the white oval on to form the body and complete the puppet.

Jack Frost

Your child can paint the windows with this mixture to make it look like Jack Frost has just paid a visit. When you wish, you can clean the window off with a wet cloth. Supervise your child closely so that he does not ingest any of the mixture.

Activity for an individual child

AGE GROUP: 18–40 months

DURATION OF ACTIVITY:
45 minutes

YOU WILL NEED:
- 5 tablespoons Epsom salts
- 1 cup beer
- Sponge
- Facial tissue or paper towels

1. Dissolve the Epsom salts in the beer. It should foam. Let this sit for ½ hour before using.

2. While you are waiting, clean off a window that your toddler can easily reach.

3. Your child can dip the sponge into the mixture and swirl it onto the window.

4. Pat the designs gently with wet tissues or paper towels.

5. When the painting dries, the salt crystals will sparkle, giving the window a frosted appearance.

Snow Dough

When it is too cold to go outside, your child can make this dough and then create a wintry landscape or fun snow creatures.

Activity for an individual child

Variable Yield

AGE GROUP: 18–40 months

DURATION OF ACTIVITY:
10 minutes

YOU WILL NEED:
- 2 parts flour
- 1 part salt
- Water
- White tempera powder paint
- White glitter

1. Mix all the flour and salt together.

2. Gradually add water until you reach the desired consistency.

3. Sprinkle in the white tempera powder and glitter for color and effect.

Snowy Picture

Here is a special way to create a seasonal picture. Perhaps you and your child can think of other ways to create a snowy effect.

Activity for an individual child

AGE GROUP: 30–40 months

DURATION OF ACTIVITY:
15 minutes

YOU WILL NEED:
- White tempera paint
- Shallow pie tin
- Small paper doilies
- Dark-colored construction paper
- Old toothbrush

1. Pour the paint into the pie tin.

2. Have your child arrange the doilies on the paper and paint over them to create snowflake patterns. Remove and discard the doilies.

3. Let your child dip the bristles of the toothbrush into the paint. Show him how to flick the bristles over the paper to splatter the paint for a snowy effect. Be sure he holds the brush far from his eyes.

Ice Cube Painting

This is a fun craft and science activity all in one. If you don't have the paint, you can also use Kool-Aid or Jell-O powder.

Activity for an individual child or a group

AGE GROUP: 18–40 months

DURATION OF ACTIVITY:
15 minutes

YOU WILL NEED:
- Ice cube tray
- Craft sticks or small tongue depressors
- Powdered tempera paint
- Construction paper or poster board

1. Make a tray of ice cubes. Freeze each cube with a craft stick sticking in so that you have a square Popsicle.

2. Let your child sprinkle the powdered paint on the paper.

3. Show your child how to use the ice cube on a stick as a paintbrush. The colors will swirl as the ice melts.

Snow Castle

Tired of snowmen? Why not pretend you're at the beach? Your child can even paint the completed castles by spraying them with a mixture of water and tempera paint or food color.

Activity for an individual child

AGE GROUP: 18–40 months

DURATION OF ACTIVITY:
20 minutes

YOU WILL NEED:
• Sand pails
• Small shovels and spoons
• A snowy day

1. Show your child how to fill the bucket with snow. Have him dump it over and mold a castle from snow.

Rainbow Melt

Your child will enjoy watching the colors run as he learns a little bit about science, too.

Activity for an individual child

AGE GROUP: 18–40 months

DURATION OF ACTIVITY:
25 minutes

YOU WILL NEED:
• Salt
• Food coloring in various colors
• Paper cups
• Ice (cubes or large block)
• Shallow pie tin

1. Mix 1 tablespoon of salt with a few drops of food coloring and put into a paper cup. Repeat process for different colors.

2. Place the ice in the pie tin.

3. Let your child sprinkle the colored salt liquid over the ice. Discuss what happens. Encourage him to observe how the colors run when the ice melts.

Groundhog Puppet

Here's a cute puppet variation. Help your child imagine an entire story around the groundhog that she creates.

Activity for an individual child

AGE GROUP: 30–40 months

DURATION OF ACTIVITY:
10 minutes

YOU WILL NEED:
- 1 small paper cup
- Tempera paint
- Scissors
- 1 piece of brown felt
- Fine-tip black marker
- White craft glue
- 1 craft stick

1. Have your child decorate a paper cup for the burrow. When the paint is dry, poke a hole in the bottom of the cup.

2. Cut a quarter-sized circle from the felt to make a head for the puppet. Your child can draw the face on with the marker.

3. Help your child glue the groundhog head onto the craft stick. Turn the cup upside down and push the bottom of the stick into the hole you made in the cup. Your child can push the stick up from the inside of the cup to make the groundhog pop up.

Find Me in the Snow

This activity will help your child develop the visual discriminatory skills she needs for reading. Be sure to use this opportunity to talk about camouflage and how it can protect an animal. You can use either magazine clippings or make your own animal outline shapes from white bond paper.

Activity for an individual child

AGE GROUP: 18–40 months

DURATION OF ACTIVITY:
10 minutes

YOU WILL NEED:
- Scissors
- White bond paper
- White craft glue
- 1 sheet white poster board

1. Cut the shapes of a number of white animals (polar bear, lemming, snow hare) from the paper and glue to the poster board.

2. Challenge your child to find the animals hiding in the snow.

Hibernation Party

Here is a fun and concrete way to teach your child about hibernation.

Activity for an individual child or a group

AGE GROUP: 30–40 months

DURATION OF ACTIVITY:
30 minutes

YOU WILL NEED:
- Snack food
- Blankets and pillows

1. Explain to your child that some animals hibernate for the winter and that today you are going to pretend to be bears and hibernate.

2. In order to have energy, you need to eat well before hibernating. Serve the child a nutritious snack.

3. Have your child help you set up a cozy bear den. You can do this by draping a blanket over a table. Use extra pillows and blankets to make the den a comfortable place.

4. Turn out the lights and encourage your child to curl up inside the den and pretend to sleep. Perhaps she can snore loudly like a bear!

5. After a short time, turn on the lights and announce that spring is here!

6. Remember that when bears emerge from their den, they do a lot of stretching. They may even be a bit hungry again!

Spring

Springtime is a time of change. Consider taking your toddler for a walk to observe the first signs of spring. Look for budding trees, birds returning from the south, the first signs of early flowers such as crocuses, and more.

Clothespin Butterfly

Painting the wings of this butterfly is a great way to talk about colors and let your child choose his favorites!

Activity for an individual child

AGE GROUP: 18–40 months

DURATION OF ACTIVITY:
15 minutes

YOU WILL NEED:
- Coffee filter
- Watercolor paints
- Clothespin
- Pom-poms (if your child is old enough not to put things in his mouth)
- Glue
- Markers

1. Have your child paint the coffee filter "wings." When dry, pinch the filter in the middle and cinch it with the clothespin. Fan out the filter so the wings show.

2. Glue pom-poms onto the top of the clothespin to represent the body. If you're not using pom-poms, just draw the body with markers.

Wind Sock

When your child is done with this project, be sure to hang it somewhere it can catch the wind.

Activity for an individual child

AGE GROUP: 18–40 months

DURATION OF ACTIVITY:
20 minutes

YOU WILL NEED:
- Crayons or markers
- 1 large sheet poster board
- Masking tape
- Hole punch
- Yarn or twine
- Crepe or tissue paper

1. Have your child use crayons or markers to decorate both sides of the poster board.

2. Roll the board into a cylinder and tape it securely on the edges.

3. Punch a hole at one end and attach a yarn loop for hanging.

4. Let your toddler tape strips of the crepe or tissue paper to the other end.

Hairy Head

With this activity your toddler can use his creative expression and learn a bit about science, too.

Activity for an individual child

AGE GROUP: 24–40 months

DURATION OF ACTIVITY:
15 minutes

YOU WILL NEED:
- Styrofoam cup
- Markers
- Potting soil
- Grass seed

1. Place the cup upright and have your child draw a face on the cup with the markers.

2. Help your child fill the cup with potting soil and plant the grass seed.

3. As the seeds grow, their cup face will have hair.

Blossom Trees

Although they will not smell as nice as real flowering trees, you will be surprised how realistic these trees look. If you don't want to use popcorn, you can have your child make little blossoms by crumpling up small pieces of tissue paper or Kleenex.

Activity for an individual child or a group

AGE GROUP: 18–40 months

DURATION OF ACTIVITY: 15 minutes

YOU WILL NEED:
- Brown crayon
- Light-colored construction paper
- White craft glue
- 1 cup popped popcorn

1. Have your child use the crayon to draw a tree trunk and branches on the paper.

2. Show your child how to glue the popcorn on the branches to make the blossoms. It works best if he puts a dab of glue on the paper rather than on the popcorn kernel.

Egg-Carton Tulips

This creative craft can be used for a festive centerpiece.

Activity for an individual child or a group

AGE GROUP: 30–40 months

DURATION OF ACTIVITY: 25 minutes

YOU WILL NEED:
- Scissors
- Egg carton (cardboard works better than Styrofoam)
- Paintbrush
- Tempera paint
- Pipe cleaners or chenille sticks

1. Cut the carton into individual egg cups.

2. Let your toddler paint the cups.

3. When the paint is dry, use the scissors to poke a small hole in the bottom of the cups.

4. Thread a pipe cleaner through each one. Pull enough of each into the center to twist a small loop. This will keep it secure as a stem and create a little stamen. Always be sure that there are no sharp wires on the ends of the pipe cleaners.

Soufflé Flowers

This simple activity results in a craft with a nice fragrance that lasts a long time. Perhaps your child will want to make a whole bouquet.

Activity for an individual child or a group

AGE GROUP: 30–40 months

DURATION OF ACTIVITY: 15 minutes

YOU WILL NEED:
- Paper baking cups or mini soufflé cups
- Watercolor paints
- Paintbrush
- Perfume
- Cotton ball
- White craft glue
- Pipe cleaner

1. Show your toddler how to open and spread the baking cups out.

2. Let your toddler paint the cups.

3. Help your child dab a small amount of perfume onto the cotton ball. When the paint is dry, he can glue the ball into the center of the flower.

4. Help your child attach the pipe cleaner to make a stem for the flower.

Summer

Here are a few activities to celebrate summertime. Remember that the most valuable way for your toddler to learn about summertime is through experience. Take the time to watch clouds roll by, go for a walk in a meadow, or drink homemade lemonade under the shade of a big tree.

Pool Noodle

These pool flotation devices can be just as much fun when used out of the pool.

Activity for an individual child

AGE GROUP: 18–40 months

DURATION OF ACTIVITY:
10 minutes

1. Option #1: Use the noodle as a limbo stick. Encourage your child to go under it as you lower it toward the ground. You can also have her jump or climb over it.

2. Option #2: Let your child balance the noodle in different ways, such as on her outstretched palm or on her head.

Spray Chalk

Your toddler needs many outlets for expressing himself. Chalk is a fun and creative art material. Your child can spray this on the sand at the beach or even on snow.

Activity for an individual child

Makes ½ cup

AGE GROUP: 18–40 months

DURATION OF ACTIVITY:
10 minutes

YOU WILL NEED:
- 1 cup water
- 4 tablespoons cornstarch
- 3 drops food coloring

1. Mix all the ingredients and put into spray bottles.

Sunflowers

This cheery craft will brighten up any summer day. Children seem drawn to these giants of the flower world.

Activity for an individual child or a group

AGE GROUP: 18–40 months

DURATION OF ACTIVITY: 15 minutes

YOU WILL NEED:
- Marker
- Brown, yellow, and green construction paper
- Scissors
- White craft glue
- Sunflower seeds

1. Draw a circle on the brown paper and the outline of eight yellow triangles on the yellow paper. Make the circle as big or small as you want the sunflower to be. Size the triangles so that side by side, they will go all the way around the circle. Cut a stem from the green paper.

2. Either cut the shapes out yourself, or assist your child in doing so.

3. Show your child how to glue the pieces together to create a flower. When the flower is dry, she can glue on the sunflower seeds in the middle.

Sun on a Stick

This project makes a cute decoration to place into a potted plant. It can also be used as a puppet or a handheld fan.

Activity for an individual child

AGE GROUP: 18–40 months

DURATION OF ACTIVITY: 15 minutes

YOU WILL NEED:
- Scissors
- 2 paper plates
- Yellow and orange tempera paint or crayons
- White craft glue
- Craft stick

1. Cut a big circle from the center of one paper plate.

2. Have your child paint or color the circle orange. Have her paint or color the intact plate yellow.

3. Help your child glue the orange circle onto the yellow plate.

4. Glue the craft stick onto the bottom to serve as a handle.

Everlasting Sand Castle

Bring the beach home with this unique craft activity.

Activity for an individual child

AGE GROUP: 18–40 months

DURATION OF ACTIVITY:
20 minutes, plus 3 days to dry

YOU WILL NEED:
- 4 cups sand
- 2 cups cornstarch
- 1 tablespoon plus 1 teaspoon cream of tartar
- 3 cups hot water

1. Mix all ingredients together and let cool.

2. Your child can use the mixture to build a castle by hand, or she can use shallow plastic containers for molds. Coat the containers with Vaseline before using.

3. Give the castle 3 days to dry.

Flowery Window Clings

Decorate any sunny window with this easy project.

Activity for an individual child

AGE GROUP: 18–40 months

DURATION OF ACTIVITY:
15 minutes

YOU WILL NEED:
- Scissors
- Clear contact paper
- Flower blossoms and leaves

1. Cut 4" squares of clear contact paper.

2. Help your child place flower blossoms and leaves on the sticky side of the paper. Leave enough of the contact paper uncovered that it will stick to the window.

3. Carefully pick up the squares and press on the window.

4. When you choose to take the flowers off the window, you can remove the excess adhesive with nail-polish remover.

Chapter 16
Holiday Activities

New Year's Day

Your young child will probably be fast asleep long before the clock strikes midnight. But she can still participate in some of the festivities. This is a great time to talk to her about the passage of time.

New Year's Noisemakers

Your child will enjoy making noise and helping to celebrate the new year without having to stay up until midnight.

Activity for an individual child

AGE GROUP: 18–40 months

DURATION OF ACTIVITY:
10 minutes

YOU WILL NEED:
- Pencil
- Toilet paper tube
- Scissors
- Waxed paper
- Masking tape
- Crayons

1. Use the pencil to poke three holes on one side of the tube. Make holes in a straight line and leave at least 1" between them.

2. Cut a square of waxed paper large enough to cover the opening of the tube. Help your child secure the waxed paper over the end of the tube nearest the hole with a long piece of masking tape.

3. Let your child decorate the horn with crayons. Show her how to blow into the horn to make noise.

New Year's Party Hat

You can adapt this basic craft and let your child make a hat for any special occasion.

Activity for an individual child

AGE GROUP: 18–40 months

DURATION OF ACTIVITY:
15 minutes

YOU WILL NEED:
- 2 sheets construction paper in bright colors
- Stapler
- Crayons
- Scissors
- Glitter
- White craft glue

1. Place the two pieces of paper together lengthwise so that they overlap by ½". Staple them together.

2. Roll the paper into a cone, making sure that the bottom is wide enough to fit your child's head. Overlap the paper at the seam and mark seam with a crayon.

3. Unroll the paper and cut off any excess.

4. Spread the paper flat and let your child use crayons and glitter to decorate one side of the paper.

5. Roll the paper back into a cone and staple it to create the hat.

Celebration Picture

Here is an unusual way for your child to create a festive picture.

Activity for an individual child

AGE GROUP: 18–40 months

DURATION OF ACTIVITY:
10 minutes

YOU WILL NEED:
- Tempera paint
- Pie tins
- Paper noisemakers
- Construction paper or poster board
- Confetti

1. Pour the paint into the pie tins.

2. Have your child dip the curled-up end of the noisemaker into the paint.

3. Show your child how to aim the noisemaker at the paper and have her blow. The goal is to have the painted tip of the noisemaker strike the paper and leave a mark.

4. While the paint is still wet, your child can sprinkle some confetti onto her picture.

Pot Banger

The classic stereotype is true: Toddlers love to bang on pots and pans. New Year's is the time to make a little noise anyhow, so why not have your child use a special pot-banging spoon?

Activity for an individual child

AGE GROUP: 18–40 months

DURATION OF ACTIVITY:
30 minutes

YOU WILL NEED:
- Tempera paint
- Pie tins
- Paintbrushes
- Wooden kitchen spoon
- White craft glue
- Glitter
- Ribbon (optional)

1. Pour the paint into the pie tins. Let your child paint the spoon however she wishes.

2. When the spoon is completely dry, show her how to coat the spoon with glue and then add glitter.

3. If you wish, tie a ribbon around the handle.

Valentine's Day

Love is in the air! Your toddler is just starting to learn about love and relationships. At this stage in his life, your toddler's greatest love is probably you. But soon, his social world will be expanding. Talk about love and caring while you do these projects with him. Here is a great chance to reinforce recognition of the colors pink and red, too.

Heart Prints

This activity will help your child develop fine motor skills. You may also want to use this as an opportunity to talk about color and shape identification. You don't have to limit your child to a simple sheet of paper. Perhaps she can print hearts onto a card or calendar.

Activity for an individual child

AGE GROUP: 18–40 months

DURATION OF ACTIVITY:
15 minutes

YOU WILL NEED:
- Red and pink tempera paint
- Pie tins
- Scissors
- Kitchen sponges
- Clothespins
- White construction paper or bond paper

1. Pour the paint into the pie tins.

2. Cut out heart shapes from the sponges. You can make other shapes too. Be sure that the sponge shapes are at least as large as a silver dollar.

3. Attach a clothespin to the back of the sponge. This will serve as a handle for your child.

4. Show your child how to dip the sponge hearts into the paint and then press them onto the paper to create a design.

Puffy Paint Hearts

This activity can introduce the idea of emotional self-expression while asking your child to be creative, too.

Activity for an individual child

AGE GROUP: 18–40 months

DURATION OF ACTIVITY:
20 minutes

YOU WILL NEED:
- 1 cup flour
- ½ cup salt
- ¼ cup water
- 4 tablespoons poster or
  tempera paint
- Pie tins
- Paintbrushes
- Paper
- Pencil

1. Mix all of the ingredients together and pour into pie tins.

2. Either you or your child can draw heart outlines on paper in a creative design.

3. Have your child paint inside the hearts. The puffy paint will add an interesting texture to the creation.

Kisses

This activity will be particularly enticing if you have a child who likes to put on Mommy's makeup.

Activity for an individual child

AGE GROUP: 30–40 months

DURATION OF ACTIVITY:
10 minutes

YOU WILL NEED:
- Lipstick in a variety of colors
- White construction or bond
  paper
- Facial tissue

1. Help your child apply the lipstick.

2. Show your child how to kiss the paper to make lip prints. If you use more than one color of lipstick, help your child use the tissue to remove the preceding color.

Valentine's Card

Here is a cute idea for your child to create a truly personalized Valentine's Day card.

Activity for an individual child

AGE GROUP: 18–40 months

DURATION OF ACTIVITY:
10 minutes

YOU WILL NEED:
- 1 sheet of white or pink construction paper
- 1 marker
- Red tempera paint
- Shallow pie tin

1. Fold the paper in half to create a card. On the front, write "Thumbody Loves You!"

2. Pour a small amount of the paint into the pie tin. Help your child dip her thumb into the paint.

3. Open the card and show your child how to press her thumb onto the paper to create prints. Let her make as many thumbprints as she wishes to decorate the card.

St. Patrick's Day

It is said that anyone can be Irish on St. Patrick's Day. Focus on the color green and share some of the legends and lore of this holiday with your child.

Living Shamrock

This is a fun gardening activity, but it takes patience to see the result.

Activity for an individual child

AGE GROUP: 18–40 months

DURATION OF ACTIVITY:
15 minutes

YOU WILL NEED:
- Scissors
- Kitchen sponge
- Water
- Shallow pie tin
- Grass seeds

1. Cut the sponge into a shamrock shape.

2. Fill the pie tin with enough water to cover the bottom. Place the sponge in the water.

3. Help your child sprinkle the grass seeds onto the wet sponge.

4. Place the pie tin with the sponge in a sunny place. Keep the sponge moist while the grass is sprouting.

Rainbow's End

This cute craft makes a pretty centerpiece for a holiday party. Add some gold-foil chocolate coins for extra excitement.

Activity for an individual child

AGE GROUP: 30–40 months

DURATION OF ACTIVITY:
15 minutes

YOU WILL NEED:

- Scissors
- Toilet paper tube
- Black felt-tip marker
- Paper plate
- Crayons or colored markers
- White craft glue
- Gold sequins

1. Cut the toilet paper tube in half crosswise. Discard one half.

2. Have your child color the half tube black to make the pot.

3. Cut the paper plate in half. Discard one half.

4. Cut off the rim of the plate to create an arch shape. You may need to trim the width a bit so that one end will fit into the "pot."

5. Encourage your child to color the arch with rainbow colors. Keep in mind that your child's creative rainbow may not resemble the real thing; that is okay.

6. Let your child glue some gold sequins to the rim of the little black pot.

7. Balance the rainbow arch by inserting one end of it into the pot opening.

Pot-of-Gold Hunt

You will be promoting your child's creative problem-solving skills while he plays this fun game. If you wish, you can substitute a real treat basket for the paper pot of gold; just be sure to decorate it with plenty of cut-out gold coins!

Activity for an individual child

AGE GROUP: 30–40 months

DURATION OF ACTIVITY:
20 minutes

YOU WILL NEED:
- Scissors
- Colored construction paper
- Masking tape

1. Cut the following shapes out of construction paper: 20 tiny green feet, 1 brown kettle, 10 small yellow circles, and an arch shape with different colors to form a rainbow.

2. Tape the yellow circles in the kettle shape to create the pot of gold.

3. Find a location to "hide" the pot of gold. Place it or tape it anywhere you wish.

4. Tape the green feet a few feet apart to form a path for your child to follow. Let them wind up the wall or under furniture to finally lead to the pot of gold.

5. Tell your child about how it is believed that a leprechaun can lead you to a pot of gold at the end of the rainbow. Show him the footprints, and encourage him to follow them to the treasure.

Passover and Purim

Both of these holidays occur in the spring. and they both celebrate the Jewish people's freedom from oppression. These activities will help you introduce the history of Judaism and its culture to your toddler.

Elijah's Cup

During the Passover Seder, an extra cup of wine is left out for the prophet Elijah.

Activity for an individual child

AGE GROUP: 18–40 months

DURATION OF ACTIVITY:
15 minutes

YOU WILL NEED:
- One large plastic wine glass
- Scraps of tissue paper
- Glue
- Ribbon

1. Let your child glue tissue scraps on the cup.

2. When the cup is dry, tie a ribbon around the stem.

Purim Gragger

Purim graggers are the noisemakers that children shake when the name of Haman is mentioned during the reading of the Megillah. Be mindful that the loose beans could be a choking hazard; supervise the use of this toy carefully.

Activity for an individual child

AGE GROUP: 18–40 months

DURATION OF ACTIVITY:
15 minutes

YOU WILL NEED:
- White craft glue
- Scraps of paper and ribbon
- 2 paper cups
- ¼ cup dried beans
- Masking tape

1. Let your child glue paper and ribbon to the outside of the cups for decoration.

2. When the glue is dry, help her pour the beans into one of the cups.

3. Invert the second cup over the first and tape together.

Matzo Cover

Let your toddler create a beautiful item that can be part of your holiday tradition for years to come.

Activity for an individual child

AGE GROUP: 24–40 months

DURATION OF ACTIVITY:
25 minutes

YOU WILL NEED:
- A white linen handkerchief or fabric remnant
- Colored tissue paper
- Spray bottle filled with water

1. Have your toddler tear the tissue paper into bits.

2. Show him how to arrange the bits on the handkerchief to create a design.

3. Let him spray the paper with water. The color will soak through.

4. Gently remove the paper and let the handkerchief dry.

Earth Day

It is not too early to start teaching your child to respect the Earth and the environment. These simple activities are a great way to start.

Litter Eater

This creative craft will make picking up litter lots of fun. It is a good idea to preclean the area and remove any hazardous materials like glass or rusty metal first.

Activity for an individual child or a group

AGE GROUP: 18–40 months

DURATION OF ACTIVITY:
45 minutes

YOU WILL NEED:
- One large plastic jug
- Scissors
- Scraps of tissue paper or ribbon
- Glue

1. Cut a hole in the front of the jug large enough for your child to insert her hand.

2. Encourage your child to decorate the jug. She may wish to make the hole appear to look like a mouth.

3. Show your child how to pick up litter and insert it into the mouth.

Recycled Critters

There is no end to materials that you can use for this project. Ask your friends and family to save things that you could use for this project, which encourages divergent thinking.

Activity for an individual child

AGE GROUP: 30–40 months

DURATION OF ACTIVITY:
20 minutes

YOU WILL NEED:
- A variety of recycled containers and objects such as: margarine tubs, toilet paper tubes, tissue boxes, lids, oatmeal canisters, buttons, soda bottles, and fabric scraps
- Glue or tape
- Colored construction paper
- Markers or crayons

1. Rinse out any containers, remove labels, and check for sharp or loose parts.

2. Have your toddler glue or tape items together to create a creature.

3. Provide paper and markers or crayons for him to decorate.

4. Be sure to ask your toddler about what he made. Where does it live? What does it eat? Does it have a name?

Easter

There are many symbols and traditions associated with this holiday. Easter eggs and the Easter Bunny may be the two most familiar to young children. Here are some simple activities that your toddler is sure to enjoy.

Footprint Bunny

Both you and your child will delight in this cute holiday craft. Don't worry if the end result does not look perfect—your child's creativity is more important than the finished result.

Activity for an individual child

AGE GROUP: 30–40 months

DURATION OF ACTIVITY:
15 minutes

YOU WILL NEED:
- White and pink construction paper
- Pencil
- Scissors
- White craft glue
- Cotton ball
- 6 (3") lengths of dark-colored yarn
- Crayons

1. Have your child stand on a piece of white construction paper in stocking feet. Trace the outline of her foot.

2. Cut out the foot shape. Cut out two long ears from the pink paper.

3. Show your child how to make a bunny: glue the ears onto the heel end of the cut-out foot and the cotton ball to the toe end.

4. Let your child decorate her bunny with the yarn and crayons.

Easter Egg Dye

You do not have to rely on a store-bought kit to dye Easter eggs. Here are some creative ideas for you to try.

Activity for an individual child

AGE GROUP: 18–40 months

DURATION OF ACTIVITY:
15 minutes

YOU WILL NEED:
- Eggs
- Coffee cups
- ½ cup of boiling water
- 1 teaspoon of vinegar
- ½ teaspoon of food coloring

1. In a coffee cup, combine ½ cup of boiling water, 1 teaspoon of vinegar, and ½ teaspoon of food coloring. Repeat this process for each color.

2. You can also make natural dyes. Natural dyes require the eggs to soak for much longer, sometimes as long as overnight. Remember the longer the egg is in the dye, the darker the color will be. Some materials to try include onion skins, beet juice, and tea leaves.

Fourth of July

Your toddler is too young to understand the history behind this holiday. Keep it simple, and explain that you are celebrating the country's birthday. Your child will love being a part of the festivities.

Handmade Flag

Let your child express his patriotism with this personalized version of the American flag. You can adapt this craft for any flag with stars.

Activity for an individual child

AGE GROUP: 18–40 months

DURATION OF ACTIVITY:
15 minutes

YOU WILL NEED:
- White craft glue
- 3 sheets white construction paper
- 1 sheet blue construction paper
- Scissors
- 2 sheets red construction paper
- White tempera paint
- Shallow pie tin

1. Glue the white and blue papers side by side to form a large square, with the blue square in the top left corner.

2. Cut (or help your child cut) the red paper into ten strips. Glue six of the strips together end to end to create three long stripes. Glue the red stripes to the white part of the square, with the longer stripes at the bottom.

3. Pour some white paint into the pie tin. Help your child dip his hands in the paint, and then press his hands on the blue square to make stars. (Don't try for all fifty; instead, you're just going for the effect.)

Halloween

You may or may not choose to celebrate Halloween with your young child. Toddlers have a great deal of difficulty understanding the difference between fact and fantasy, so common symbols and sights of this holiday can be truly frightening for them. Giving your child hands-on, safe opportunities to explore scary things can help her understand and feel more in control.

Egg-Carton Bat

Popular culture has done much to malign the reputation of bats. Most bats are harmless and even helpful in keeping the insect population in check. You can talk to your child about bats while you do this craft.

Activity for an individual child

AGE GROUP: 30–40 months

DURATION OF ACTIVITY:
15 minutes

YOU WILL NEED:
- Scissors
- 1 cardboard egg carton
- Black tempera paint
- Red tempera paint
- Small paintbrushes
- Black construction paper
- White craft glue

1. Cut off one cup of the egg carton. This will be the bat's body.

2. Let your child paint the cup black and then use the red paint to add facial features.

3. While the paint is drying, cut out two wings from the construction paper. Each wing should be no longer than 2" long.

4. Show your child how to glue the wings onto the bat.

Spaghetti Monsters

This cute craft will stimulate her imagination and help with mastery of fear.

Activity for an individual child

AGE GROUP: 18–40 months

DURATION OF ACTIVITY:
10 minutes

YOU WILL NEED:
- 2 handfuls cold cooked spaghetti noodles
- Tempera paint
- Pie tins
- Construction paper
- Glue
- Miscellaneous scraps of fabric, buttons, googly eyes, and so on

1. Have your toddler grab a handful of noodles and dip them into the paint.

2. Ask her to lay the mound of noodles onto the paper.

3. Remove the noodles to leave the paint impression.

4. When the paint is dry, have her decorate her monster however she wishes.

Tissue-Paper Ghosts

This is such a simple activity with a very cute result. Your child may want to make a lot of ghosts and then hang them around the house for decoration.

Activity for an individual child

AGE GROUP: 30–40 months

DURATION OF ACTIVITY:
10 minutes

YOU WILL NEED:
- Tissue paper such as Kleenex
- Cotton balls
- Masking tape
- Yarn cut into 12" sections
- Fine-tip black marker

1. Show your child how to drape the sheet of tissue paper over the cotton ball.

2. Help your child secure the cotton ball by wrapping a piece of masking tape tightly below. This will form the neck. If you wish to hang the ghost later, stick a piece of yarn under the tape.

3. Your child can use the marker to draw on the eyes and mouth. Hang the ghost where the breeze will catch it and make it fly.

Paper-Plate Spiders

Even if your child is afraid of spiders, he is still likely to enjoy this cute craft.

Activity for an individual child

AGE GROUP: 30–40 months

DURATION OF ACTIVITY:
15 minutes

YOU WILL NEED:
- Crayons
- 2 paper plates
- Hole punch
- 2' of yarn
- White craft glue
- 8 strips black construction paper

1. Let your child color the front of the plates. He can draw in a face for the spider if he wishes.

2. Punch a hole in the center of one of the plates. Knot the end and thread the yarn through the hole from front to back. This will be used to hang the spider.

3. Help your child glue the black strips onto the back of one plate. These are the spider's legs—they should be evenly spaced and should stick out past the rim of the plate.

4. Glue the two plates together back to back to complete the spider.

Masks

Masks can be particularly frightening for a young child, who may not recognize the transformed face as someone she knows and may not understand that the transformation is temporary. This activity may help your child overcome any fear, but if she is reluctant to wear the mask, then don't force her.

Activity for an individual child

AGE GROUP: 18–40 months

DURATION OF ACTIVITY:
15 minutes

YOU WILL NEED:
- Scissors
- Paper plate
- Crayons and markers
- White craft glue
- Craft stick
- Mirror

1. Cut wide holes in the paper plate to make eyes and a mouth.

2. Have your child decorate the back of the plate to create a face.

3. Glue the craft stick onto the bottom to serve as a handle. Your child can then hold up the mask to her face. Let her see herself in a mirror.

Spider Webs

Your toddler will enjoy making this unusual craft.

Activity for an individual child

AGE GROUP: 18–40 months

DURATION OF ACTIVITY:
15 minutes

YOU WILL NEED:
- White craft glue
- Shallow bowl
- 1 cup cooked spaghetti, cooled
- Waxed paper

1. Pour some glue into the shallow bowl.

2. Show your child how to dip each noodle individually into the glue. Have her hold the noodle over the bowl to let any excess glue drip off.

3. Let her arrange the noodles onto the waxed paper in her version of a cobweb design.

4. When the design is dry, you can lift it off the paper and hang it from the ceiling.

Thanksgiving

The history of this holiday is more than your child can understand. Discussions about Pilgrims and Native Americans are not relevant to your child's experience of the world around her. The turkey, on the other hand, is a concrete symbol of the Thanksgiving meal. You may also choose to have a discussion about abundance and thankfulness during this holiday.

Pumpkin Pie Dough

Here is fun seasonal dough. Your toddler can pretend to be a cook right alongside you and create fun dessert shapes and more, but be warned that it does not taste as good as it smells!

Activity for an individual child

Makes 2 cups

AGE GROUP: 18–40 months

DURATION OF ACTIVITY:
20 minutes

YOU WILL NEED:
- 5½ cups flour
- 2 cups salt
- 8 teaspoons cream of tartar
- ¾ cup oil
- 1 ounce pumpkin-pie spice
- Orange food coloring
- 4 cups water

1. Mix all the ingredients together over low heat.

2. Stir constantly until mixture reaches the consistency of mashed potatoes.

3. Remove from heat. When cool, knead.

Turkey Trap

Engage your child's imagination with this activity. This may become a family tradition for years to come.

Activity for an individual child

AGE GROUP: 18–40 months

DURATION OF ACTIVITY:
15 minutes

YOU WILL NEED:
- 1 cardboard box
- 1 sturdy stick
- A few kernels of corn
- Feathers
- Candy corn

1. Tell your child that you are going to trap a turkey for Thanksgiving.

2. Set the cardboard box upside down and prop up one end with the stick. Show your child how the turkey will knock the stick over to make the box fall. Place some corn under the box to serve as bait.

3. Overnight, remove the corn and replace it with the feathers and candy corn. If you want, you can add a little note/poem from the turkey:

YOU TRIED TO CATCH ME, BUT I CAN'T BE BEAT.
SO I LEFT SOME CANDY FOR YOU TO EAT!

Thanksgiving Tablecloth

Your toddler will feel that she is truly contributing to the holiday when she helps make this festive tablecloth.

Activity for an individual child
or a group

AGE GROUP: 18–40 months

DURATION OF ACTIVITY:
20 minutes

YOU WILL NEED:
- 1 large light-colored flat sheet (white or yellow works best)
- Black fabric marker
- Fabric paints

1. Spread the sheet somewhere with plenty of room for your child to work.

2. Have your child place her hand on the sheet, palm down, with her fingers spread wide. Trace around her hand with the fabric marker. Repeat to create as many turkeys as she wishes. Perhaps the rest of the family will add their turkeys as well.

3. Allow her to use the fabric paint to embellish the turkeys and to add any other decoration that she wishes.

Chanukah

Chanukah is a Jewish holiday steeped in tradition. Don't forget to share some of your favorite ways to celebrate with your young child. This holiday lasts for eight days. Here are a few favorite activities to get you started with the celebration.

Handprint Menorah

This activity is a great way to reinforce Jewish holiday traditions as well as introduce your child to counting concepts.

Activity for an individual child

AGE GROUP: 30–40 months

DURATION OF ACTIVITY:
15 minutes

YOU WILL NEED:
- Washable blue and yellow tempera paint
- 2 pie tins
- 1 sheet construction paper

1. Pour the paint into separate pie tins. Have your child dip his hands in the blue paint and then press them flat onto the paper. His thumbs should overlap while his fingers should be spread apart.

2. Show him how the print resembles a menorah, with the thumbprints representing the Shamash. Count the eight candles with him.

3. Wash your child's hands. Then have him dip one finger into the yellow paint. Help him press his finger over each candle to make a flame.

Wooden Star of David

Your child will be learning about shapes and geometry while he makes this well-known symbol.

Activity for an individual child

AGE GROUP: 18–40 months

DURATION OF ACTIVITY:
20 minutes

YOU WILL NEED:
- 6 craft sticks
- White craft glue
- Blue and white tempera paint
- 2 shallow pie tins
- Paintbrushes

1. Show your child how to arrange three craft sticks to form a triangle. Have your child glue these sticks together. Repeat for a second triangle.

2. Once dry, show your child how to place one triangle upside down over the other triangle to create the Star of David. Glue the triangles in place.

3. Let the star dry. Pour paint into pie tins and let your child decorate the star.

Tube Menorah

With this menorah, you can add all of the flames at once or have your child add a flame on each night of the holiday.

Activity for an individual child

AGE GROUP: 30–40 months

DURATION OF ACTIVITY:
20 minutes

YOU WILL NEED:
- Scissors
- 8 toilet paper tubes
- 1 paper towel tube
- 1 piece of cardboard 8" × 11"
- White craft glue
- Holiday gift wrap scraps
- Yellow or orange tissue paper

1. Cut 4 (¼"-long) slits on one end of each tube. Fold these tabs back. Arrange the tubes on the cardboard—the tall tube in the center and four smaller tubes on each side. Glue in place.

2. Have your child glue the wrapping paper on the tubes for decoration. Encourage him to make the tall one (Shamash) stand out from the others.

3. Show your child how to crinkle a square of the tissue paper and stuff it into the top of a tube to represent a candle flame. Start with the center candle and do the same for all of the others.

Christmas

Even your young toddler will be aware of the hustle and bustle of the Christmas season. It is hard to shelter her from the music, the commercials, the movies, the decorations, and everything else. She does not have to be a passive bystander, though. These activities will encourage her to contribute festive decorations for your home.

Hanging Ornaments

This is a simple way to create attractive ornaments. You may also use plastic lids, although it is harder to punch a hole in them.

Activity for an individual child

AGE GROUP: 18–40 months

DURATION OF ACTIVITY:
15 minutes

YOU WILL NEED:
- Hole punch
- Lids from frozen juice cans (be sure there are no sharp edges)
- Pieces of yarn
- Glitter, sequins, stickers, tinsel
- White craft glue

1. Punch a hole ½" in from the edge of each lid. String and loop a piece of yarn so that your child can hang her ornament.

2. Have your child decorate both sides of the lids with the glitter and craft materials.

Dough Ornaments

There is no limit to what your child can imagine and create with this project. This clay hardens in the oven. The ornaments will continue to smell heavenly for quite a while.

Activity for an individual child

Makes 3 cups

AGE GROUP: 18–40 months

DURATION OF ACTIVITY: 45 minutes

YOU WILL NEED:
- 1½ cups flour
- 1½ cups cinnamon and nutmeg mix
- 1 cup salt
- 1 cup water
- Holiday cookie cutters
- 1 straw
- Ribbon for hanging

1. Mix all the ingredients together. Add more water if dough is dry and does not hold together.

2. Have your child knead the dough and then roll it out into a disc ¼" thick.

3. Show your child how to cut out shapes from the dough using cookie cutters. Before baking, use the straw to cut out a small circle at the top of each ornament for the ribbon.

4. Bake for 30 minutes at 350°F and let cool before trying on a ribbon and hanging.

Lacy Balls

You will be surprised at the elegant and delicate appearance of these ornaments. Remember that balloon pieces can be a choking hazard for young children; only an adult should pop the balloon and discard the pieces.

Activity for an individual child

AGE GROUP: 18–40 months

DURATION OF ACTIVITY: 1 hour

YOU WILL NEED:
- Plastic bowl
- ⅓ cup white craft glue
- ⅔ cup liquid laundry starch
- Lengths of yarn 1"–7" long
- Small inflated balloon

1. In the bowl, mix the white craft glue with the liquid laundry starch.

2. Show your toddler how to dip yarn into this mixture and drape around the blown-up balloon.

3. Have her repeat with additional yarn strands until a desired pattern or design is created. She should leave some gaps and not cover the balloon completely.

4. Once the yarn is dry, pop and remove the balloon.

Handprint Wreath

This is a personalized holiday decoration. You may wish to do one with each member of your family.

Activity for an individual child

AGE GROUP: 30–40 months

DURATION OF ACTIVITY:
25 minutes

YOU WILL NEED:
- Scissors
- Paper plate
- Green and red construction paper
- Pencil
- White craft glue

1. Cut the flat center out of the paper plate so that only the rim remains.

2. Have your child spread her fingers and lay her hand flat on the green construction paper. Trace around your child's hand with the pencil to create a hand template.

3. Cut out a dozen hands from the template.

4. Cut out three red circles, about the size of a grape.

5. Help your child arrange the hands around the plate ring. You want the hands to overlap and the fingers to reach outward.

6. Help your child glue the hands to the plate. Let her glue on the red "berries" for a finishing touch.

Kwanzaa

Take this opportunity to share with your young child the heritage and history of African Americans.

Kwanzaa Colors

Here is a simple way to introduce your child to the traditional colors of Kwanzaa.

Activity for an individual child

AGE GROUP: 18–30 months

DURATION OF ACTIVITY:
15 minutes

YOU WILL NEED:
- White craft glue
- Water
- Paper cup
- Paintbrush
- Green and red tissue paper
- Black construction paper

1. Mix the glue with a small amount of water in a paper cup. The glue should be thin enough to paint on the paper with a brush.

2. Let your toddler tear the tissue paper into shreds.

3. Have him lay out the tissue paper on the black construction paper.

4. Help him paint over the tissue paper with the glue solution. Be careful he does not saturate the paper so much that it is soaked through.

Kwanzaa Placemat (Mkeka)

This is a personalized holiday decoration. You may wish to do one with each member of your family.

Activity for an individual child

AGE GROUP: 30–40 months

DURATION OF ACTIVITY:
20 minutes

YOU WILL NEED:
- Black, green, and red construction paper
- Scissors
- Masking tape
- Clear adhesive contact paper

1. Fold a piece of black construction paper in half crosswise.

2. Cut slits from the folded center to about 1" away from the edge. Space the slits 1" apart. Unfold the paper.

3. Cut out red and green strips just a little thinner than 1" and as long as the black paper.

4. Help your child weave the strips through the black paper. Alternate the red and green strips and be sure to push each one snug against the previous one. Don't worry if the pattern is not perfect.

5. Secure any loose ends with the tape. Cover in contact paper to use as a placemat.

Chapter 17
Party Time

Theme Parties

You don't need to have a fancy theme to have a successful birthday party for your child. But there are advantages to a theme party. It may be easier for you to decorate and plan for a party that revolves around a theme. You can adapt just about any menu or activity to fit your theme. For example, the game Pin the Tail on the Donkey can fit into any of the themes below if you simply change it to Pin the Ears on the Teddy Bear, Pin the Nose on the Clown, or Pin the Tiara on the Princess!

Circus Theme Party

There are many fun ways to celebrate a circus theme. If you are considering inviting an entertainer for the party, keep in mind that many toddlers are afraid of clowns.

Activity for a group

AGE GROUP: 18–40 months

DURATION OF ACTIVITY:
1 hour

1. Let the children put on their own circus. Set out three hula hoops for the rings. Invite each child to take a turn stepping inside the ring to dance or perform.

2. Stretch a thick rope on the ground and challenge the guests to walk along it as if they were in a high-wire act.

3. No circus is complete without face painting. You will find a recipe in Chapter 12.

Teddy Bears' Picnic Theme Party

This is a great theme idea for an outdoor party.

Activity for a group

AGE GROUP: 18–40 months

DURATION OF ACTIVITY:
1 hour

1. Encourage children to bring their own teddy bears to join in the festivities. Be sure to have a few extra on hand for those who attend the party without one.

2. Weather permitting, serve refreshments outside on a picnic blanket. One themed menu idea is Teddy Grahams.

3. Put on some music and have guests dance with their teddy bears. They can also form a circle by holding hands with each other and the bears to play Ring Around the Rosy.

4. You can create simple party hats for your guests. Create a headband from folded brown construction paper. Cut out brown bear ears for the children to glue on.

Princess Theme Party

Make your birthday girl feel special and make her princess for a day.

Activity for a group

AGE GROUP: 18–40 months

DURATION OF ACTIVITY:
1 hour

1. Let your guests get into character by making some props, such as crowns and magic wands. Be creative!

2. Be sure to have some old dresses and fancy accessories for the party guests to play dress-up.

3. Before your guests sit down at the table for refreshments, have them decorate folding chairs to create their own thrones. Provide each child with an old pillowcase. Cut off half of the length. Let the children decorate the pillowcase with fabric paints. When they are dry, simply slip the covers on the backs of the chairs to create thrones.

Birthday Party Activities for Two-Year-Olds

Your child's second birthday will not hold much meaning for him. Recognize that children this age often have difficulty playing together. Have different options on hand that will let your young guests play on their own if they are not ready to join the group.

Birthday Blocks

Not all birthday games need to be group activities. Two-year-olds often do best when simply playing side by side. Here is a fun play activity to have available.

Activity for an individual child or a group

AGE GROUP: 18–40 months

DURATION OF ACTIVITY:
15 minutes

YOU WILL NEED:
- Scissors
- Tape
- Gift wrap
- Wooden building blocks
- Clear contact paper

1. Use scissors and tape to wrap each building block like a miniature gift. Cover them in contact paper to keep the wrapping paper intact. Give the blocks to the children to build with.

Follow the Path

You will need a fairly large space for this activity. Be sure that children are supervised so that they do not pick up the rope and tangle it around a playmate or themselves.

Activity for a group

AGE GROUP: 18–40 months

DURATION OF ACTIVITY:
15 minutes

1. Use a thick rope or cord to create a path for the children to follow. The more twists and turns you can make, the better. You can tape or weigh down sections of the rope to make them stay put.

2. Set up a surprise at the end of the path, such as a basket of party favors or the birthday cake.

Birthday Party Activities for Three-Year-Olds

For your child's third birthday, you can plan more involved activities. Children of this age have a longer attention span and are better able to follow directions.

Party Hats

Skip the store-bought party hats. Your guests will enjoy making their own.

Activity for an individual child or a group

AGE GROUP: 30–40 months

DURATION OF ACTIVITY:
20 minutes

YOU WILL NEED:
- Construction paper
- Stickers
- Ribbons and bows
- Confetti
- White craft glue
- Stapler

1. Let each child choose a sheet of colored construction paper. Have them decorate one side with stickers, ribbons, bows, and confetti.

2. When the paper is dry, you can fit the hat for each child. Roll each piece of paper into a cone so that the opening fits on the child's head. Staple the cone closed along the seam.

Flour Bombs

This is strictly an outdoor activity and makes a fun alternative to water balloons. You may wish to set up a target or just let the children bomb the trees, pavement, and walls.

Activity for an individual child or a group

AGE GROUP: 30–40 months

DURATION OF ACTIVITY:
15 minutes

YOU WILL NEED:
- Paper napkins
- Flour
- Masking tape

1. For each flour bomb, fill ½ of a paper napkin with flour. Bring up the ends of the napkin and twist. Secure the bomb with a little bit of masking tape.

Group Craft Projects

A group craft project can be a fun way to involve all of the party guests, young and old alike. These activities focus more on the process than on the finished project.

Giant Mural Puzzle

The nice thing about this activity is that the guests get to take puzzle pieces home with them, and you get to see what a group of kids does when asked to be creative together. You may want to provide smocks, as this can be a messy activity.

Activity for a group

AGE GROUP: 18–40 months

DURATION OF ACTIVITY:
30 minutes

YOU WILL NEED:
- Butcher paper
- Pie tins or pans
- Tempera paints
- Large paint brushes
- Scissors

1. Hang a large sheet of butcher paper in a place all the children can easily reach. Outdoors is best.

2. Give the children pans of tempera paint and large brushes. Encourage them to work together to paint a large mural.

3. You want children to work together, but if you notice territorial battles, it is best to intervene. You can solve most problems by marking sections of the mural off with a pencil.

4. When the children are done, let the painting dry.

5. Cut the paper into equal sections, enough to give one to each child.

6. Distribute the sections and then challenge the children to put the mural puzzle back together again.

Homemade Wrapping Paper

You can let the children take some of the paper home. Alternatively, do this project at the beginning of the party and while the children are preoccupied with something else, have someone use this paper to wrap the party favors.

Activity for a group

AGE GROUP: 18–40 months

DURATION OF ACTIVITY: 20 minutes

YOU WILL NEED:
- Scissors
- Kitchen sponges
- Butcher paper
- Tempera paint
- Pie tins
- Wooden clothespins

1. Before the party, cut the sponges into different shapes such as a party hat or birthday cake. If you are having a theme party, cut shapes that match the theme.

2. Seat your guests around a table covered with butcher paper.

3. Pour different colors of paint into the pie tins and show the children how to use the sponges as stamps. Attach the clothespins to the sponges if children are having difficulty grasping the sponges.

4. Encourage the children to create a design on all areas of the paper. Let dry before dividing or using.

Fence Tapestry

This is a great project if you have a cyclone fence (a.k.a. a chain-link fence) in your yard. You will be surprised at how nice the finished result looks. Be sure to take pictures of the completed results to send home. Supervise this project carefully, and be mindful of any materials that could pose a choking hazard.

Activity for a group

AGE GROUP: 18–40 months

DURATION OF ACTIVITY: 30 minutes

YOU WILL NEED:
- Various weaving materials, such as ribbons, foil scraps, newspaper strips, twigs, yarn, and old sheets or curtains

1. Show the children how to weave the different materials through the fence holes. The weaving technique does not have to be perfect or uniform. In fact, it will look better when children add materials in their own way.

More Party Games

Here are more all-purpose party games. You will find that they are appropriate for a wide range of ages and abilities. They require few materials and little planning for those times when you need a little something extra to pass the time.

Blob Race

Although relay races may be too complex for young children, they will enjoy this simplified version.

Activity for a group

AGE GROUP: 30–40 months

DURATION OF ACTIVITY: 20 minutes

1. Divide the guests into two teams. Designate a starting and a finish line for the race.

2. On your signal, teams are to race to the finish line. The one rule is that all members must stay connected. You can have them run different heats with variations. They can form a train, hold hands, or make a giant hug circle. See what other ideas they can dream up.

Silly Says

Here is a simplified version of Simon Says. In this adaptation, the leader is not trying to "trick" anyone.

Activity for a group

AGE GROUP: 18–40 months

DURATION OF ACTIVITY: 20 minutes

1. Start the game with an adult as the leader to show the children how it is played. Then each child can take a turn being the leader.

2. The leader picks out a character to imitate and calls out the directions using that persona ("Dora says" or "the Easter Bunny says").

3. The leader tells the group what to do (jump, spin, or touch their noses).

Sleeping Lions

As with many other activities in this chapter, you can adapt this game to meet the theme of your party.

Activity for a group

AGE GROUP: 18–40 months

DURATION OF ACTIVITY:
15 minutes

1. Divide the guests into two groups. One group is the lions; the other group is the safari photographers.

2. Instruct the lions to lie down and pretend to be sleeping.

3. The photographers are to sneak up as close as they can to take a picture without waking the lions.

4. When the lions awaken, they are to roar and scare away the other group.

5. Make sure that all children get a turn to be in both groups.

Party Preparation and Props

As any party host knows, half the fun of having a party is in the anticipation and planning. Don't be afraid to involve your child and to let her make some small choices and decisions about her special day. Encourage her to participate in the preparation.

Napkin-Holder Place Cards

Here is a creative way to involve your toddler in the party preparations.

Activity for an individual child

AGE GROUP: 18–40 months

DURATION OF ACTIVITY:
20 minutes

YOU WILL NEED:
- Scissors
- Wrapping paper or tissue paper
- Toilet paper tubes
- White craft glue
- Stickers
- Felt-tip marker
- Address labels

1. For each napkin holder, cut a piece of wrapping paper or tissue paper to fit around the tube.

2. Help your toddler glue the paper onto the outside of the tube.

3. Let her attach decorative stickers on each tube.

4. Write the guest's name on the address label and affix it to the tube.

5. Roll and insert a colorful napkin.

Table Centerpiece

Let your child's imagination shine through—she'll be proud that her creation is on display at the party.

Activity for an individual child

AGE GROUP: 18–40 months

DURATION OF ACTIVITY:
30 minutes

YOU WILL NEED:
- 2 sheets construction paper
- Empty coffee can
- White craft glue
- Scissors
- Colored tissue paper
- Shallow pie tin

1. Help your child roll the sheets of construction paper to cover the outside of the coffee can. Let her glue the paper on.

2. Trim off any extra paper.

3. Let your child rip the tissue paper into tiny squares.

4. Show your child how to crumple up each square to create a tiny ball or blossom.

5. Pour a small amount of glue into the pie tin.

6. Have your child dip each tissue wad into the glue and stick it onto the can.

7. When your child is done decorating the can in this fashion, let it dry.

8. Use the container to hold flowers or balloons.

Party Photo Frames

What better party favor than a reminder of all the fun times!

Activity for a group

AGE GROUP: 18–40 months

DURATION OF ACTIVITY:
30 minutes

YOU WILL NEED:
- Scissors
- Poster board
- Felt-tip marker
- Confetti
- Glitter
- White craft glue
- Instant or digital camera

1. For each frame, cut a square of poster board 2" larger than the diameter of the picture you will be using.

2. Cut out a square from the center of the poster board, leaving a 1½" frame.

3. Use the marker to write a title on the top of the frame, such as "Tony's Second Birthday Party."

4. Let each child decorate her own frame with the confetti and glitter.

5. Take and print the pictures while the frames are drying. You can take a picture of each child separately, or assemble the children in a group. Don't push for perfect smiles or wait for everyone to be looking in one direction. Let them be a little silly and capture the true fun they are having.

6. Attach a photo behind each frame with a small dab of glue or rubber cement.

Index